THEODORE M. HESBURGH

THEODORE M. HESBURGH
A Bio-Bibliography

Compiled by
Charlotte A. Ames
with a Biography by Thomas Stritch

Foreword by Theodore M. Hesburgh C.S.C.

Bio-Bibliographies in Education, Number 1

Greenwood Press
New York • Westport, Connecticut • London

Library of Congress Cataloging-in-Publication Data

Ames, Charlotte A.
   Theodore M. Hesburgh : a bio-bibliography / compiled by Charlotte
A. Ames, with a biography by Thomas Stritch ; foreword by Theodore
M. Hesburgh.
      p. cm. — (Bio-bibliographies in education, ISSN 1044-7962 ;
no. 1)
   ISBN 0-313-26508-9 (lib. bdg. : alk. paper)
   1. Hesburgh, Theodore Martin, 1917- . 2. University of Notre
Dame—Presidents—Biography. 3. Hesburgh, Theodore Martin, 1917—
Bibliography. 4. University of Notre Dame. Archives.
I. Stritch, Thomas. II. Title. III. Series.
LD4112.7 1952 .A74   1989
378.772'89—dc20   89-38277

British Library Cataloguing in Publication Data is available.

Library of Congress Catalog Card Number: 89-38277
ISBN: 0-313-26508-9
ISSN: 1044-7962

First published in 1989

Greenwood Press, Inc.
88 Post Road West, Westport, Connecticut 06881

Printed in the United States of America

The paper used in this book complies with the
Permanent Paper Standard issued by the National
Information Standards Organization (Z39.48-1984).

10 9 8 7 6 5 4 3 2 1

In Gratitude

to

Reverend Theodore M. Hesburgh, C.S.C.

Contents

Foreword by Theodore M. Hesburgh

I am deeply grateful to Charlotte Ames and her many collaborators (recognized in her Acknowledgments) for this superb and comprehensive work. I have to confess to having forgotten many of the articles chronicled here. Seeing them all brought back many happy and some unhappy memories. Most of the writing was occasioned by the challenges I was facing at the moment: how to forge ahead during the difficult civil rights revolution, how to feed the hungry worldwide, how to create a new life for refugees, how to confront the specter of nuclear war, how to tame nuclear power and convert it to peaceful uses, how to use science and technology for better development in the Third World. But throughout all of these continuing crises, there was the persistent challenge of higher education: how to strive continually for quality while enlarging equality for all, particularly minorities; how to balance science and the humanities, how to insist on values, the most difficult dimension in all education; how to emphasize the international implications of all this.

Anyway, these have been good years, despite the failures that were interspersed with the successes. One is grateful for the successes and wiser for the failures. Above all, one is determined to keep trying because there will never be a dearth of problems and, at its best, education is at the heart of most solutions.

May I offer a special word of thanks to my old friend and colleague, Professor Thomas Stritch, who has provided an honest, compassionate and, if anything, too kind minibiography that leaves me deeply in his debt, and also determined to try harder to be as good as he portrays me. Again, one must keep trying.

My persistent reaction to reading all of this is: Don't take yourself too seriously. There is still a lot to be done, or as Robert Frost put it, we all have promises to keep and miles to go before we sleep.

(Rev.) Theodore M. Hesburgh, C.S.C.
President Emeritus
University of Notre Dame

Preface

Theodore M. Hesburgh: A Bio-Bibliography consists of
three major sections: a biography of Father Hesburgh prepared
by Thomas Stritch, Professor Emeritus of American Studies,
University of Notre Dame; a description of archival and
manuscript materials held in the Archives of the University
of Notre Dame prepared by William Kevin Cawley; and a
bibliography of Father Hesburgh's major published and
unpublished works, as well as selected works about him.

Since he became president of the University of Notre
Dame in 1952, Father Hesburgh has gained international
recognition and reputation as one of the most respected and
influential leaders in the American Catholic Church. Through
his vision, vitality, and unflagging zeal, Father Hesburgh
has wrought profound change in countless areas of universal
concern. His magnanimous contributions to Church and state
are clearly evident in his deep commitment to advancing the
cause of Catholic education, and in his passion for ensuring
the protection and preservation of all human rights. He has
been widely honored for his extraordinary service as priest,
educator, university president, and public servant.

The bibliographical section of this volume includes
works by Father Hesburgh issued from 1940 through mid-
February 1989. Published works include books; articles and
essays; forewords, prefaces and introductions; newspaper
articles; interviews; selected United States government
documents; and non-print media. Unpublished works include
addresses, papers, speeches, and diaries. Works about Father

Hesburgh consist mainly of books, articles, and newspaper articles of both a biographical and a reportorial nature. Theses and dissertations as well as works which contain relevant sections of information about Father Hesburgh are also included under books about him.

ARRANGEMENT

Each entry in the bibliography has been assigned an item number. Within each chapter, citations are arranged chronologically by date of publication, from the earliest to the most recent. Within each year, entries are arranged alphabetically by author, or by title if no author has been specified. Father Hesburgh's published addresses are cited according to the date of publication of the work, not by the date on which he delivered an address. When an article or an address has been published in several sources, usually the first appearance of the work has been cited, with references to subsequent printings.

The Archives of the University of Notre Dame is the official repository for Father Hesburgh's papers. As such, it holds an enormous wealth of material pertaining to Father Hesburgh's life and work which has not been cited in this bibliography. More than one hundred unpublished sermons, speeches, and addresses, many of them dating from the years of his early priesthood, as well as more recent unpublished works are available in the Archives of the University of Notre Dame, but not listed in this bibliography. A vast quantity of manuscript and printed material relating to Father Hesburgh's work with various organizations, as well as photographs, artifacts, and non-print media are available in the Archives. William Kevin Cawley, Archivist, has prepared a detailed and comprehensive description of archival holdings which appears in the chapter entitled Archives and Manuscripts.

To indicate the location of some works cited, the following codes have been used:

The Archives of the University of Notre Dame: UNDA.

The Department of Public Relations and Information,
    University of Notre Dame: UDIS.

Various subfield codes following the code UNDA signify
designations used by the Archives for their internal
retrieval purposes. When materials cited from the Archives
or the Department of Public Relations and Information have
not been found elsewhere, the location code has been
indicated.

Most government documents issued under corporate
authorship and published by the United States Government
Printing Office are listed under Documents. To facilitate
access to some government publications, the Superintendent
of Documents number (SuDoc no.) has been provided. Materials
which may be obtained from ERIC (Educational Resources
Information Center), an educational information service,
include an ERIC number, e.g., ERIC ED 092 786. Documents
related to Father Hesburgh's work which were issued by the
International Atomic Energy Commission and other agencies are
generally listed under Unpublished Works. They are
available in the Archives of the University of Notre Dame.

Various communiqués, such as letters to presidents of
the United States, or to parents of Notre Dame students
regarding student protests and campus unrest, have been
listed under Unpublished Works. Interviews issued as journal
or newspaper articles are cited under Interviews. Interviews
which have been issued as sound recordings or videorecordings
are listed under Non-print Materials. An OCLC (Online
Computer Library Center) number has been cited for some non-
print materials to facilitate retrieval of bibliographic
information. A comprehensive listing of documentaries and
interviews prepared by major television networks has not been
included.

With reference to newspaper articles, a wealth of
material exists in the news media covering all periods of
Father Hesburgh's career. With few exceptions only selected
articles reporting significant events or major statements
have been included. Researchers are encouraged to consult
appropriate newspaper indexes such as the *New York Times*, the
Los Angeles Times, the *Washington Post*, the *Chicago Tribune*,

Newsbank Electronic Indexes, the *Catholic Periodical and Literature Index,* and similar sources for additional information regarding Father Hesburgh's activities in academic, religious, and government affairs.

METHODOLOGY

In order to provide a fairly comprehensive listing of works by and about Father Hesburgh, citations were prepared for selected works found in three distinct locations at the University of Notre Dame: The Archives of the University of Notre Dame, the Department of Public Relations and Information, and the Theodore M. Hesburgh Library. In addition, both manual searches and online database searches of various indexes have contributed significantly to the content of this bibliography. Citations to selected items appearing in several Notre Dame publications such as the *Notre Dame Magazine,* the *Scholastic,* and the *Observer* (the Notre Dame student newspaper) have been included. Further references may be obtained by consulting appropriate volumes of these and other Notre Dame publications, such as the *Dome*; the *Alumnus*; the *Notre Dame Report,* the Institute for International Peace Studies *Newsletter,* general histories of the University of Notre Dame, and other publications.

The Theodore M. Hesburgh Civil Rights Collection contains an extensive array of various types of documents pertaining to Father Hesburgh's work on the United States Civil Rights Commission. William R. Valentine's *Directory: Theodore M. Hesburgh Civil Rights Collection,* published in 1976, provides a comprehensive listing of civil rights materials, many of which have not been included in this bibliography. Selected works from Valentine which have been cited provide a small sampling of the type of material which is listed in Valentine's *Directory.* The notation "Valentine," followed by an item number, e.g., Valentine no. 5565, facilitates access to the microfilm copy. The entire collection is available on microfilm in the Archives of the University of Notre Dame.

During the course of his career, Father Hesburgh has received well over one hundred honorary degrees from academic institutions in the United States, Canada, and abroad. With few exceptions, all institutions were contacted for copies of addresses which he may have given on these occasions. Bibliographic citations have been included for most commencement addresses which are available.

Throughout his writings, Father Hesburgh has frequently visualized the reality of the Catholic university, the ideal Notre Dame, as a beacon, bridge, and crossroads "where all the vital intellectual currents of our times meet in dialogue . . . ." On a somewhat different scale, in an entirely different key, perhaps this bio-bibliography may be considered a beacon, bridge, and crossroads to Father Hesburgh's life and work.

Charlotte A. Ames

Acknowledgments

While it is impossible to express my thanks individually to
all those who have assisted in this work, words of sincere
appreciation are rendered to Rev. Theodore M. Hesburgh,
C.S.C., for his very valuable contributions; to Helen H.
Hosinski for her invaluable service; to Dr. Wendy Clauson
Schlereth, University Archivist, for her kind assistance in
providing technical support; to Dr. William Kevin Cawley,
Archivist, for his detailed description of archival holdings,
and for his expertise in computer technology which has made
this work a reality. To Richard W. Conklin and his staff in
the Department of Public Relations and Information, to Sister
Elaine V. DesRosiers, O.P., and her staff in Educational
Media, and to many others in the Notre Dame community and
elsewhere who have provided support in a myriad of ways, I am
especially grateful.

Among the many individuals from the Theodore M. Hesburgh
Library who have assisted in this project, I am indebted to
Robert C. Miller, Director of Libraries, and to the Friends
of the Library for their sustaining support. Words of
special thanks go to Maureen L. Gleason, Assistant Director
for Collection Development and Coordinator of Technical
Services, for her wise counsel and kind encouragement.
G. Margaret Porter, Database Services, has been extremely
helpful in providing online database searching for many
years. Linda Gregory and the staff in Interlibrary Loan;
Pamela J. Paidle and the staff in Current Periodicals and
Microtext Reading Room; Mollie H. Toole, Collection

Development; and Stephen M. Hayes, Government Documents, have been most accommodating in a variety of ways. Others who have been particularly helpful include the late John J. Philippsen; Sylvia Frost; Beth Picknally; Mary Windhorst; David E. Sparks; Laura S. Fuderer; Rafael E. Tarragó; Susan E. Saavedra; Mary R. Cowsert; Lorenzo A. Zeugner, Jr.; Alan Krieger; Katharina J. Blackstead; and student assistants Katie Clark, Danielle Bafile, and Paul Savage.

Many other individuals in the University Libraries and the Notre Dame Law School Library have also contributed significantly to the preparation of this work, and their kind assistance is deeply appreciated. To the countless librarians, archivists, and other individuals throughout the United States and abroad who have contributed so generously of their time, talent, and expertise, I am forever grateful.

THEODORE M. HESBURGH

A Short Biography of
Theodore M. Hesburgh by Thomas Stritch

Theodore Martin Hesburgh, president of the University of
Notre Dame from 1952 to 1987, may well be the American
Catholic priest who has caught and kept public interest for
longer than any other. His tenure as president of the
university whose image he changed is the longest in
contemporary U.S. higher education. Some older university
presidents have had longer ones, notably Charles Eliot of
Harvard (1869-1909) and Nicholas Murray Butler of Columbia
(1902-1945). Eliot was fond of saying that a college president's
name is writ in water, but Hesburgh's seems graven in more
durable stuff.

Hesburgh's influence begins at home with the university
he headed for so long. His accomplishments there are
formidable. Foremost is his money-raising. Under his
leadership Notre Dame's endowment rose from $10 million to
more than $450 million, from nowhere to twenty-first among
the nation's private universities. Under him the Notre Dame
campus spread eastward in a cascade of new buildings,
creating a campus almost as large as the original one, while
enlarging and renovating the old campus without changing its
unique character. Average faculty salaries soared from
$5,400 to $50,000, well past inflation and student tuition.
Enrollment nearly doubled, from 5,000 to 9,600. The yearly
operating budget zoomed from $9 to $200 million, as Notre
Dame went co-ed and changed over to lay governance from
control by its founding religious community of Holy Cross.

But the main Hesburgh achievement lies in the new prestige he brought to Notre Dame. Whatever its merits--and they were considerable--the Notre Dame Hesburgh took over in 1952 simply did not have the prestige of the Notre Dame of 1987, when he retired. Hesburgh inherited a college that had just turned the corner to university status. He left it a full-fledged university, on its way to the top. Notre Dame, already well-known for its football splendors, gradually became well-known for its academic ones, and Hesburgh, in an era when college presidents came and went like professional baseball managers, became the best-known college president in the United States. There had been vision and promise before Hesburgh. But now the circumstances were ripe. By 1952 Notre Dame was ready, and Hesburgh was its prophet.

As if this were not career enough, Hesburgh has played a significant role in national affairs. This story is well told in the late Kingman Brewster's introduction to the printed version of Hesburgh's Terry Lectures, delivered at Yale when Brewster was its president and published under the title *The Humane Imperative* in 1974:

In international conciliation he has raised his colleagues out of the ruts of self-interest--in the international control of the peaceful uses of atomic energy, and in the mobilization to help poorer nations and peoples, especially in Africa and Latin America. Father Hesburgh's contribution to the continuing and unfinished effort to make the Declaration of Independence and the Bill of Rights a living reality for all Americans is so widely appreciated that it needs no embellishment. This ideal of equality has been kept alive, and its achievement is still a realistic hope, in considerable part because of Father Hesburgh's strenuous, stalwart championship of the cause of human dignity and equality. This reached a new and critical importance when the tide of the civil rights struggle began to ebb; hope for millions would be more forlorn if it were not for his steadfastness . . . . This quality [of] spirituality is Father Hesburgh's very special gift to those over whom he presides, those to whom he

ministers, and those for whom he writes and speaks.
There is no passivity in his contemplation, since the
realization of God's will demands that the person throw
all of himself into the cause. There is no gloom in his
dedication, since it is sustained by a confidence that
the Holy Spirit is at work in us all, in the world, and
in the cosmos.

This extraordinary language reflects the high esteem the
academic community in the United States has for Hesburgh,
which has earned him a record high 114 honorary degrees
(Herbert Hoover is second with 89). Responsible American
journalism echoes these sentiments. *The Nation* magazine
called Hesburgh "the most influential cleric in America."
Hesburgh has been on a *Time* magazine cover, and the subject
of an admiring magazine article by Fred Hechinger, the long-
time education editor of the *New York Times.* On the whole,
without trying but with a keen sense of its usefulness to his
enterprises, Hesburgh has had an excellent press, particularly
in television. Even student journalism, ordinarily the worst
ordeal a university president has to endure, has been nearly
always respectful, and often proud and cheering. As for
Hesburgh himself, he has said that he was troubled early on
by the requests made for his services to the national weal,
but as soon as he realized that his educational and civil
goals were basically the same he welcomed public service. He
often seemed to court trouble, at Notre Dame and in Washington,
but he nearly always came through unscathed, the smiling
survivor, a Daniel among the tractable lions.
    The well-named Theodore ("Gift of God") Hesburgh was
born in Syracuse, New York, on May 25, 1917, into a family
not quite typical in American Catholicism, but by no means
unusual. His father was of German descent, his mother, Anne
Marie Murphy, Irish. But she was schooled in New York City
by nuns mostly of German descent, and so was no Irish ghetto
product. A lively and intelligent lady, she made a happy
home for her husband and five children.
    Hesburgh's father and paternal grandfather were both
named Theodore. Grandfather Theodore Bernard was a
schoolteacher and journalist, presaging the career of his

famous grandson. As Father Ted himself might have done,
Grandfather Theodore, writing for the *New York World*, Joseph
Pulitzer's paper, opposed Archbishop Michael Corrigan, New
York's testy Catholic leader, for suspending the ardent
supporter of Henry George, Father Edward McGlynn, from his
priestly duties. Journalist Hesburgh argued not so much for
the righteousness of the George Single-Tax Program as for the
freedom of clerics to take part in political life: a clear
anticipation of Father Ted's passionate defense of academic
freedom.

Hesburgh's father had a much different sort of life.
When he was three years old the flu epidemic of 1891 carried
off his mother, brother, and sister. His distracted father
took him to live with some distant relations on a farm in
Iowa, but seven years later he was rescued by an aunt who
brought him back to New York. But life was never easy for
Theodore Bernard. He worked at all sorts of odd jobs to help
earn his keep, and managed somehow to graduate from high
school, which was by no means taken for granted in his day.
He then started to work for the Pittsburgh Plate Glass
Company, where he remained for the rest of his business life,
gradually climbing up the ladder until he became manager of
its warehouse in Syracuse. His children remember him as a
hard worker as well as a sincere and deeply religious man,
devoted to his job and his family. In later life he and his
wife contributed to the redecoration of the crypt of Sacred
Heart Church at Notre Dame, where Father Ted celebrated mass
every day he was at the university.

Father Ted was the second of the five Hesburgh children.
A younger brother, James, is a Notre Dame graduate and a
successful businessman in California. One sister, Mrs.
Robert O'Neill, lives in Cazenovia, New York, and another,
Mrs. John Jackson, in Syracuse. A third died young, in 1957.
The Hesburgh family was normal American middle class. Young
Ted grew up an altar boy, a Boy Scout, a builder of model
airplanes, a typical American boy. He was a good student
and, with the rest of his family, devoted to the Church and
its pious practices. Very early on, at about age 12, he
determined to become a priest and was attracted to the
religious orders. At first he thought about becoming a

Jesuit, but then he met and admired a Holy Cross Father, Thomas Duffy, and, influenced by Duffy, decided to join the Fathers of the Holy Cross.

The Congregation of Holy Cross is named after the little town of Saint Croix, near Le Mans, France, where it was founded in 1837. It is a community of priests, brothers, and nuns, one of many such begun in the early nineteenth century in the wake of the French Revolution. This spiritual movement is one of the most striking events in recent Catholic Church history. The French Revolution had attacked the Church, confiscated its property, closed its houses of study, and established a new regime based on atheism and a passionate anticlericalism. But in little more than a generation a tremendous revival of religion took place in France. Many new religious orders were formed, many older ones rejuvenated. The focus for much of this renewal was the foreign missions. In 1822 the French Societé de la Propagation de la Foi was founded. It eventually underwrote a good portion of missionary support in foreign lands. It was during this period that the French missionaries earned their reputation for being the first and best of Catholics bearing the gospel to lands that knew it not. France once again became "the eldest daughter of the Church," a soubriquet she acquired in the Middle Ages.

Holy Cross was not founded as a missionary enterprise. It was from the beginning a loose organization--an ecclesiastic "congregation," known at the outset of its history as "Auxiliary Priests." These lived together and helped out in parishes, schools, and the general work of a diocese, so that its members, priests, brothers, and eventually nuns stayed close to ordinary Catholic lay people, and bore little resemblance to the traditional orders with their long traditions and loyalties. But the French missionary spirit was strong in them, and an early recruit, Father Edward Frederick Sorin, ordained in 1838, headed for the wilds of northern Indiana. Indeed, at that time, Indians still traversed the land in greater numbers than the white men. But that was rapidly changing, and Sorin's school, named for Our Lady, superbly located near the burgeoning cities along the southern edges of the Great Lakes, steadily grew. The freewheeling style of the young Congregation of Holy Cross found ready acceptance in freewheeling America.

It was a style that exactly suited Theodore Hesburgh when he arrived at Notre Dame in the fall of 1934, although his initial reception was a frosty one. His father, mistrustful of his own old jalopy, had borrowed a car from a friend to drive his son to Notre Dame. Arriving at the seminary on Saturday, they were told to come back on Monday, when registration began officially. But once over this little mix-up, young Hesburgh throve. He spent a year in the "little" seminary at Notre Dame getting his studies in order, and then got through the severities of his year in the novitiate. Once in the Philosophy department of the seminary he quickly caught the attention of his teachers, who decided to send him to Rome to give him the best education it was then thought a priest could have. It was the custom of the Holy Cross community to send their best and brightest there.

Hesburgh landed in Rome in 1937, as Europe was bracing itself for war. He was lucky in the setup Holy Cross afforded him. The residence was run by the French wing of the community, and French was its normal lingua franca. His lectures and texts at the Gregorian University were in Latin. On the streets he heard Italian, and vacations were spent at a German spa. Thus the young Hesburgh was schooled in many tongues and acquired some facility in all of them, plus the Spanish he picked up later at Notre Dame. Three years of this gave him a cosmopolitan polish and introduced him to the urbanites of the capital of the Catholic world. Then came the war, and all the Americans came home.

To young Ted this meant finishing his studies at the Catholic University in Washington. The Holy Cross theology seminary had been established there, as part of the movement to make the university a center of Catholic studies. Theology in the United States at this time was gradually being disinterred from under the avalanche of secular positivism that had nearly buried it between 1870 and 1930. But the impact of the depression and Hitler, and above all the new thinking in physics and mathematics that shattered the assurance of the physical sciences, coupled with the distinguished new thinking in theology itself, made way for

its renewal, respect, and influence. Theologians like
Catholic Jacques Maritain and Protestant Reinhold Niebuhr
became as well known as Hemingway and the atom smashers. In
this atmosphere Theodore Hesburgh was ordained a priest in
1943 and took his doctorate in theology two years later.
Characteristically his thesis was on the practical rather
than the speculative, entitled when published by the Notre
Dame Press *The Theology of Catholic Action.*

Throughout his life he was to remain the activist, the
do-er, the cut-the-gaff-and-let's-get-going type. Although
he respected intellectual speculation, the bone and sinew of
a university, his temperament was its opposite. It was not
until he became immersed in the civil rights movement that he
reached the positions he has since held steadfastly. These
are basically two: the dignity of the person and academic
freedom.

These twin principles inform and help to shape all he
has done, in Notre Dame and out of it. They are to him no
empty rhetoric. He puts them to work on all occasions and
tests their meaning constantly, in encounters with exigent
faculty, naive students, and self-seeking careerists in
public life. If this is to be liberal, Hesburgh is a purebred
one, though by no means doctrinaire. He has never revealed
how he votes, and has served both Republican and Democratic
administrations. He does not pop off about anything and
everything. Always and above all he is a priest, careful,
measured, spiritual.

His position is best expressed in his book, *The Humane
Imperative,* whose inspired title encapsules the Hesburgh
credo. Its key signature is sounded early on, at the
beginning of the prelude: ". . . that theological and
philosophical principles can become operative in a wide
variety [of human affairs]; and that, as a result, the world
will become better, more human, even somewhat divine and . . .
godly." This cautious optimism is characteristic of Hesburgh's
entire career. It is not a rational conclusion, nor, like
his devotion to human dignity and academic freedom, rules for
action. It is more a prayer than a principle, an expression
of faith "that the Holy Spirit is at work in the world." In
the book Hesburgh hopes that the United States, with its

mixed racial heritage and its history of freedom, can lead
the world to ecumenism and to respect for the human person.
In spite of the problems of increasing population, the growth
of swollen cities, and the poverty of the Third World, the
author remains optimistic, seeing in the Green Revolution and
other technology hopeful signs of coping. The book ends with
a plea for two citizenships: one's own country and that of
the whole world.

Hesburgh's liberalism is built on freedom and autonomy.
This allegiance is almost poignantly related to his Holy
Cross community. More than a half-century before him Notre
Dame had been rent by a struggle between two opposed wings of
its members. One wing was satisfied with what they had--a
boarding school on the French model aimed at making pious and
docile Catholics out of their charges. Although the
university was spottily intellectual, bolstered by some good
research and writing here and there, it had no real
commitment to the life of the mind.

The other wing was, of course, just the opposite. Led
by two excellent scholars, it wanted to make Notre Dame first
a real, then a great, university. Foremost among them was
Father James A. Burns, who, as Provincial Superior of the
Indiana Holy Cross Province, was ultimately responsible for
sending young Hesburgh to Rome for study. Burns had spent
much of his priestly life urging able young men in his
community to go on to advanced studies. He himself had come
to scholarly eminence by an unusual route. His life at Notre
Dame began as a student in a Manual Training School, the sort
of project dear to the conservatives in the Notre Dame
community. But Burns soon progressed from there into the
chemistry laboratories of the leader of the liberal wing,
Father John A. Zahm.

Zahm came out of nowhere to become perhaps the foremost
scholar the Holy Cross community has produced, a passionate
self-taught scientist who began experimenting and writing
scholarly papers before he was ordained. From him Burns
caught the intellectual fever, though he didn't stay in the
physical sciences to which Zahm was devoted. He moved into
the fledgling field of education, and became the foremost
authority, still much quoted, on Catholic education in the

United States. These two pioneers began the revolution that Hesburgh eventually finished.

Hesburgh only gradually came to see his part in this long evolution. After his ordination he wanted to become a military chaplain, but his superiors told him to "get his ticket," as the Ph.D. is generally known in the trade. It was necessary to his career. When he came to teach theology at Notre Dame in 1946, his was the only doctorate in the department. He taught with great success, and wrote a widely used textbook, *God and the World of Man*.

He also became, in a roundabout way, the military chaplain he yearned to be. After the war Notre Dame was flooded with veterans getting their education on the G.I. Bill of Rights. For married vets, the university built a little village on the campus, by a happy coincidence where the Hesburgh Library now stands. In this odd ambience of tight quarters, steamy kitchens, drying diapers, and hard study--teaching the vets was a golden time for the faculty-- Hesburgh flourished. He became confessor, baby-sitter, confidant, and friend to hundreds of these young people, and they in turn helped to form him into a warm, compassionate, tolerant, and sympathetic person. Because of them Hesburgh identified with the students rather than the administration at Notre Dame. When, after only three years of "Vetville," the then president, Father John J. Cavanaugh, approached him to join the administration as his executive vice-president, Hesburgh's hackles bristled. He wanted no part of official discipline and officious policing.

But President Cavanaugh knew what he was doing. More than Hesburgh, he was the originator of modern Notre Dame. He set up the Notre Dame Foundation to raise money on a year-round basis, the forerunner of Hesburgh's remarkable organization. He reorganized the structure of the administration and filled it with the ablest men he could find. But most of all Cavanaugh brought Notre Dame into the mainstream of the new world that was being born in the wake of World War II. He realized that Hesburgh's vets required a new approach. They were mature men, not callow boys. Between them, Cavanaugh and Hesburgh created a new tone. Gradually the old boarding-school regulations began to be

ignored, then repealed. It was a trying time for the new
leadership.

Not until Hesburgh became president himself, succeeding
Cavanaugh in 1952, did the old regime collapse. The students
who followed the vets, rejoicing in their new freedom,
wanted, of course, to repeal all regulations, but they found
a firm Hesburgh drawing the line where he deemed it
essential. In letters to students and their parents he made
it plain that he stood for law and order, not anarchy. At
the same time he established a rewarding liaison with student
leaders and worked with them as best he could. Something in
him appealed to the students. College students are a curious
lot. Individually generous and idealistic, collectively they
can be barbarous as well as foolish. Hesburgh dealt with
them with a hand as adroit as it was sensitive. He was ready
to talk to them, visit them in their dorms, reason with them,
and above all be candid with them. Yet he never got down on
all fours with them. Always he kept a certain distance--with
Hesburgh a valuable natural trait, for he treated the faculty
and staff with the same combination of invitation and
reserve. With all he supported the instruments of freedom, a
Faculty Senate, student government with some real authority,
several varieties of journalism free for civil dissent.
Occasionally he slipped into an attitude that could be called
overbearing, and he was lucky that no incident of it became
magnified or distorted.

Although Notre Dame was not as riddled with student
rioting in the stormy 1960s as many other private schools, it
had its share of troubles. Drugs, pornography, and outrageous
student behavior--some, like the sit-ins, fairly civil, others
coarse and nasty, frequently abetted by the anarchists
usually latent in any faculty--became the undergraduates'
occupation rather than study. Like most university
presidents, Hesburgh came under considerable attack from
student press and protesters. The over-all thrust of these
was rather odd: repeated suggestion that he turn over the
running of the university to one of two or three laymen at
Notre Dame, and become himself chancellor, dealing with
national affairs. Hesburgh bore it with patience until, in
the climactic year 1968-1969, he tackled the anarchists head-

on. The heart of his message was this ultimatum:

Anyone or any group that substitutes force for rational
persuasion, be it violent or nonviolent, will be given
fifteen minutes of meditation to cease and desist. They
will be told that they are, by their actions, going
counter to the overwhelming conviction of this community
as to what is proper here. If they do not within that
time cease and desist, they will be asked for their
identity cards. Those who produce these will be
suspended from this community as not understanding what
this community is. Those who do not have or will not
produce identity cards will be assumed not to be members
of this community and will be charged with trespassing
and disturbing the peace on private property and treated
accordingly by the law.

Bold words; and the rest of the message was just as bold:

Without the law, the university is a sitting duck for
any small group from outside or inside that wishes to
destroy it, to terrorize it at whim . . . . The last
thing in the world a shaken society needs is more
shaking. The last thing a noisy, turbulent, and
disintegrating community needs is more noise,
turbulence, and disintegration . . . . Complicated
social mechanisms, out of joint, are not adjusted with
sledgehammers . . . . I have no intention of presiding
over such a spectacle . . . . Without being
melodramatic, if this conviction makes this my last will
and testament to Notre Dame, let it be so.

The tone of the message, especially the ending, shows
that Hesburgh realized he was sticking his neck out. But it
also shows he was fed up to the neck. He must have known the
message would make the national news headlines in this
apprehensive February of 1969. It did, and provoked an
avalanche of response, some of which was negative. The
student newspaper predictably urged him to resign. Others,
equally sophomoric, made the equally predictable noises about

Church authoritarianism, hauling the much-maligned Inquisition out of the sixteenth century grotesquely into the twentieth.

The bulk of the response, however, was a sigh of relief from the vast majority of Americans bewilderingly repelled by the antics of their juniors. Someone, said newspapers and magazines and broadcasts, has at last had the courage to tell these twerps off. Most of these never knew that Hesburgh was almost as troubled by the conservative response as by the protesters. It was his intervention with President Nixon and some members of the Congress that helped prevent the president from sending troops into college campuses on a national scale, compounding the mischief done earlier at university after university, and later tragically at Kent State. Nor did most students even know that Hesburgh had quietly let it be known that any student wishing to absent himself from classes in order to take part in a civil protest was to be excused.

Some of his fellow university presidents said that Hesburgh's ultimatum had no meaning for them--that only Notre Dame's homogeneous, largely Catholic student body would put up with such a ukase. Said the president of a California state college, "If we tried that, our students would burn the place down." He may well have been right. But, as the chancellor of UCLA noted, Hesburgh's example had a good deal of influence on other university administrators. Along with his civil rights crusade, his courage and example in getting the country through the turmoil of the 1960s may stand as his outstanding accomplishments for the nation at large.

One reason why Hesburgh got away with his stand was the trust the Notre Dame students had in him. Even the student journalists who called for his resignation knew that Hesburgh stood for freedom and dignity. One of them did not hesitate later to call on Hesburgh to get him out of the clutches of the Khmer Rouge when he was working for *Time* in Cambodia-- and Hesburgh did not hesitate to use his influence to help secure his release. This undercurrent of trust, this link between Hesburgh and his students never failed him. Moreover, it was based in part on Hesburgh's sympathy with some student causes, much as he deplored their lawless pursuit of them.

One of the main student causes was participation in making decisions that affected their welfare. Hesburgh, especially in the 1970s and 1980s, insisted on student representation on almost every university committee. One of the foremost student concerns was the draft. Hesburgh called for its replacement with a national service system, allowing young men to opt for the Peace Corps and such like. He roundly condemned the shooting of the students at Kent State. But his greatest scorn was reserved for the continued prosecution of the Vietnam War. "Mental midgets" was his contemptuous term for the responsible federal officials.

Surrounding all this, going both forward and backward in time, was Hesburgh's concern for raising the Notre Dame standards of academic excellence. This was his text, endlessly repeated, from the day he took office to the day he resigned it. A university, he insisted, was first of all an intellectual enterprise. Bolstered by training of character, and underpinned by religious faith, it would be a better intellectual enterprise, but neither character nor religion came first. This is a major theme in *The Hesburgh Papers*, subtitled *Higher Values in Higher Education*, published in 1979. Here he reprinted a portion of a 1967 statement issued by a number of Catholic university presidents meeting at Land O'Lakes, Wisconsin: "In a Catholic university all recognized university areas of study are frankly and fully accepted and their internal autonomy affirmed and guaranteed. There must be no theological or philosophical imperialism." On the opposite page he added: "Academic freedom, like all freedom, is grounded ultimately in the nature of man and of society and of the development of knowledge and intelligence." His annual addresses to the Notre Dame faculty stressed this and the twin theme of dedication to becoming the best.

But Hesburgh did not neglect the moral dimension. "While the community is primarily academic, I submit that its basis of unity must be of the heart as well as of the head. It was not merely intellectual problems that recently unravelled great institutions of learning across the world [referring to the disruptions of the 1960s], but rather the dissipation of moral consensus, community, and concern." This theme runs concurrently with that of academic primacy in

The Hesburgh Papers. Hesburgh emphasizes that in its warm acceptance of the world of the spiritual, Catholic education adds a dimension largely avoided in secular education. "Have no fear of commitment," he says, "as long as it is intelligent and deeply believes on real evidence the truth of those great Christian values to which *we* [my italics] are committed."

With this in mind Hesburgh labored to improve academic matters at Notre Dame. In this he had no instant success, no spectacular turnaround, no national news story. Although he found the going rough, he bore down. One of his earliest plans was the restructuring of academic departments into divisions. Like so many other college presidents, he found the traditional departments inflexible. Another red herring was his investment in television, which he thought would come to be an important, perhaps a major, force for change in university teaching. He wasn't the only one, of course; one of the enduring chimeras of U.S. education has been the substitution of pictures for teachers. Only a live teacher can adjust the pace of comprehension by a class; a film can't know, and the class can't tell it. President Hesburgh was on surer ground when he began beating the bushes for superior scholars for the faculty. With the help of George N. Shuster, a Notre Dame graduate and former professor, just resigned as president of Hunter College in New York City, he projected institutes and programs to lure distinguished scholars to Notre Dame.

The best lure, Hesburgh soon came to know, is money. This meant fund-raising, and in this he made his greatest success. He had a bonanza of good luck fairly early on, in 1960. The recently established Ford Foundation decided, as one of its top priorities, to give substantial help to some leading private universities. It picked six to help them achieve regional excellence: Johns Hopkins, Stanford, Vanderbilt, Denver, Brown, and Notre Dame. The choice of Notre Dame in such good academic company was itself a ringing affirmation of what Hesburgh had come to stand for in his eight years as president. Gone were the humiliating days of only a few years ago, when his press conferences were attended largely by sports writers. Welcome to the new day

of national recognition as the director of a leading
educational institution. Hesburgh immediately, with the help
of his staff at the Notre Dame Foundation, began a drive to
raise $12 million to qualify for the Ford grant of $6
million. It was an instant success: $24 million in all was
raised. Its focus was the new library, now appropriately
named the Theodore M. Hesburgh Library, dedicated in 1964.
Its location changed the face and character of the campus,
and its facilities heightened the quality of Notre Dame
education. The collection is still far from ideal, but the
faculty offices and the study spaces for students created a
new ambience for scholarly work.

The focus of the next drive, launched in 1963, was the
huge Athletic and Convocation Center, named in 1987 for
Hesburgh's executive vice-president and right-hand man during
all his term of office, Reverend Edmund P. Joyce, C.S.C.
Joyce was an amiable South Carolinian, of conservative
instincts and tastes. He masterminded the actual building of
the Hesburgh era, forty-eight new structures, six major
renovations, three large additions, and steady renovation.
Hesburgh has praised Joyce's work again and again. Noting
their marked differences--Hesburgh liberal, Joyce
conservative; Joyce as clever with figures as Hesburgh with
words; northern Hesburgh and southern Joyce--Hesburgh says,
"He brought to Notre Dame everything I couldn't bring to it.
I include our national reputation for an athletic program
with integrity."

During Hesburgh's first year in office Notre Dame's
phenomenally successful football coach, Frank Leahy,
resigned, ironically driven from the job by the very
intensity that made him good at it. Hesburgh's predecessor,
Father Cavanaugh, was close to Leahy, and spurred his
decision to retire, afraid that he would explode if he
didn't. Faced with the problem of choosing his successor,
Hesburgh and Joyce picked young Terry Brennan, a former
Notre Dame star and a successful high school coach in
Chicago since his graduation.

It was an engaging idea: young Hesburgh and young
Brennan, energetic, ardent, idealistic, confronting the
wolves of the college football world together. Terry did

pretty well, but not well enough for Notre Dame. After this Hesburgh left athletics largely to Joyce. But he did not, as so often accused, wash his hands of the Notre Dame athletic traditions. One of his most adroit achievements was the shift of Notre Dame's image away from football and toward academic excellence without losing football preeminence. This is an amazing feat. Some universities, on the road to academic preeminence, like Chicago, abandoned football. Others, the Ivy League notably, abandoned big-time football. Hesburgh wanted Notre Dame to be best in both. Of the original Ford Foundation grantees, only Stanford can, and does, play football with Notre Dame.

By the time the Joyce Center was dedicated, in 1968, Hesburgh and his alter ego in money-raising, James W. Frick, had perfected their organization and settled down for the long run. Frick, raised in an orphanage and befriended by Holy Cross in his nonage, had a touch of genius in raising money. First came organization, no doubt of that. But along with organization Frick tackled the problem head-on. He simply asked for money. And insisted, and demanded. There was such earnestness in him, and in his finisher, Hesburgh, such sincerity, such conviction, that they generally prevailed. Their third campaign, begun in 1967, raised $62 million, and their fourth, ending in 1982, $180 million. As with the campaign just being concluded, which is aimed at raising $300 million, these had many foci. Perhaps closest to Hesburgh's heart were the two aimed at faculty improvement, the superb Decio Faculty Office Building, and the endowment of nearly one hundred faculty chairs. The chair salaries are tops, but the average faculty salary compares well with any university in the land, around $50,000, the proud achievement of Provost Timothy O'Meara and his chief.

There is no doubt that the bedrock of Notre Dame's successful money-raising was the improved status of American Catholics. In 1920, when Notre Dame's President James A. Burns tried to raise another million dollars, in addition to the million he had previously raised with the help of grants from the Carnegie and Rockefeller foundations, he didn't make it. No doubt his failure owed something to weak organization; little was known then about money-raising.

But, looking back, a social historian might well conclude that the Catholic body simply did not have the money, just as, looking at Hesburgh's career, it's plain that it did. Of course there's more to it than that. It's like mining: getting the stuff out of the ground is just as important as knowing it's there, and it takes a great deal more talent and energy. Our social historian may well wonder if there is any private fund-raising in American history as remarkable as Notre Dame's, collegiate or otherwise.

The success at money-raising also owed a good deal to Hesburgh's own image. As president of Notre Dame, he became increasingly prominent. His invitations to serve on boards and committees were far more numerous than the ones he accepted. By the early 1970s he had become the foremost Catholic, cleric or lay, in the United States. He was acknowledged as such by the well-known Father Andrew Greeley, who said that he ought to be a cardinal. Others said he ought to be a bishop. Both were wrong. The plain fact is that the president of Notre Dame has the best Catholic position in the United States. If he can bring to the post, as Hesburgh did, charismatic qualities of mind and personality, he will be the first thought of those who turn to the Catholic Church for authority, prestige, and opinion. The post is best filled by a plain priest. Bishop, cardinal, layman, all are wrong for the job. There is a priestly dignity natural to it which makes recognition and accomplishment easier. Hesburgh's dignity, ease, and candor brought him wide acceptance especially among non-Catholics.

His first two appointments to positions of national importance came from the U.S. president of his early years in office, Dwight D. Eisenhower. The earlier, to the National Science Board, stimulated his deep interest in technology-- Hesburgh has an amateur interest in almost anything scientific. The second, however, changed his life.

This was his appointment as a charter member of the first Civil Rights Commission in 1957. Eisenhower had asked the Congress to create this commission in 1956, and he was eager to people it with the best he could persuade-- partially, no doubt, to take some of the heat off himself. Besides Hesburgh the members were Chairman John Hannah,

the former president of Michigan State; John Battle, former
governor of Virginia; Ernest Wilkins, a black who was
assistant secretary of Labor; Doyle Carlton, former governor
of Florida; and Robert Storey, former dean of the Law School
at Southern Methodist. Since there were no precedents, the
committee members themselves did work that would normally
have been entrusted to a staff--interviews with plaintiffs,
searching conversations with officials, all sorts of reports
and journalism. During these Hesburgh was deeply touched by
the stories of poor people deprived of their rights,
especially the right to vote. Then and there he became the
passionate advocate of full citizenship for all. In 1961 he
was moved to add a long addendum to the commission's report,
a special plea for racial justice.

In 1969 President Nixon made him chairman of the
commission. Fred Hechinger, the long-time education editor
of the *New York Times*, says that Nixon thought of Hesburgh as
a "pillar of the establishment, to be used by the White House
for its own purposes." If so, never was an estimation wider
off the mark. The Nixon administration, bent on putting the
brakes on the black revolution, was constantly under fire
from Hesburgh. The climax came in 1972, when Nixon proposed
antibusing legislation in the guise of the Equal
Opportunities Educational Act. Testifying before the House
Committee on Education and Labor, Hesburgh denounced the
bill: "If this measure is designed to implement the 1954
decision requiring desegregation of schools, it fails. If it
is designed to provide equal education opportunities, it
fails. If it is designed to move the nation towards justice,
it fails. But if it was designed to fractionalize the nation
along racial lines, it succeeds." He added, "This bill burns
the last bridge out of the ghetto." As John Lungren notes in
Hesburgh of Notre Dame, it burned Hesburgh's last bridge to
the Nixon administration. By the end of the year Hesburgh
was forced to resign, occasioning his famous remark, "I
suppose they will appoint some rabbit."

Partly because it solidified and confirmed his stand on
racial justice, Hesburgh regards his service on the Civil
Rights Commission as the most important of his fourteen
presidential appointments. He had a special affinity with

President Jimmy Carter, who named him to head a delegation of
eighty Americans to a United Nations Conference on Science
and Technology for Development in Vienna in 1977, carrying
the rank of ambassador. In 1979 Hesburgh accepted from
Carter the chair of the Select Committee on Immigration and
Refugee Policy, whose report advocated closing the back door
a little on illegal immigration, and opening the front door a
little on legal admissions. Earlier, as a member of
President Gerald Ford's Clemency Board, his leniency was
objected to by a board member. "I'm in the pardoning
business," Hesburgh replied, memorably.

Besides government service, Hesburgh has also been
active in many private service organizations, both religious
and secular. For many years he was on the board of the
Rockefeller Foundation, serving as its chairman for a time.
Here he devoted himself to the Green Revolution, which
brought greatly improved agricultural production to the
populous have-not nations. Hesburgh has long maintained that
the abortion-birth control controversies that have so wracked
both the public and religious sectors largely miss the point.
Developed or developing countries control their populations,
he says, while the less-developed countries do not,
irrespective of whether they are Catholic or not. Italy, he
points out, has the same low rate of population growth as
Sweden, and Spain the same rate as Russia. "I am not arguing
the moral implications of these situations," he adds,
"although I would welcome some new inspirational, spiritual
and moral approaches to human sexuality, which has been
largely taken over by the hucksters." Characteristically,
Hesburgh had thrown his energy and talent to work on a
practical help toward solving the population problem, while
realizing that it is far more complex than what is covered
through the Green Revolution.

The great global preoccupation for Hesburgh, one that
continues into his retirement unabated, is his concern for
the proper use of atomic energy, emphatically not weaponry.
As permanent Vatican representative to the International
Atomic Energy Agency in Vienna (1957-1970), he searched for
ways to turn the use of atomic energy from weapons to human
betterment, especially in the underdeveloped nations.

Harnessing atomic power to Green Revolution aims is one way, and there are others. As chairman of the Overseas Development Council, Hesburgh sought to influence U.S. foreign policy toward intelligent uses of U.S. power and money in the third and fourth worlds. Always practical, he does not rule out working with nondemocratic regimes. Universal social and economic justice must be realized bit by bit, piece by piece, working steadily upward. It won't come with a wave of ideological wands or revolutionary backlashes. Hesburgh's influence in these matters has campus implications. The new Institute for Peace Studies, financed by Mrs. Joan Kroc of McDonald's fame, is an ongoing Hesburgh concern, while the established Kellogg Institute for International Relations stresses Latin American conditions.

The interactions of all his extracampus activities with the campus, and with education, is a special satisfaction to Hesburgh. Moving hesitantly at first, he gradually became convinced that the world and national concerns to which he devoted himself were intimately tied to his goals for Notre Dame. Graduate work in government and international relations, history, theology, the sciences both physical and biological, and much else is deeply and richly connected to government and private philanthropic service. The interplay in the United States between government and science, as reflected in the National Science Foundation, has helped make the Notre Dame of Hesburgh's dreams possible. More and more the Notre Dame faculty participate in the National Endowment for the Humanities as well. These are the stuff of the modern university. The lonely scholar, typified by Goethe's Faust, is as passé as Faust's esoteric learning. The new university lies in the land where many strands converge: state, nation, world, government, religions, and a hundred other things meet and mingle in the great university. This is new, and the convergencies are often difficult and the projects ill-starred. But the vitality of this mix is what counts.

The old Notre Dame was deeply provincial, by contrast. It aimed to inculcate manners and morals. The learning was conventional and perfunctory--some Latin tags for the boys, debating and public speaking rather than scholarship for the serious, character building for all. Religion was not in the curriculum; there were no courses in religion or theology at Notre Dame until the 1920s. But moralizing was everywhere, in all the classes, in all the numerous church and chapel services, in every daily act.

Hesburgh took two important steps to open up Notre Dame for the twenty-first century. Both left old Notre Damers aghast. The first was autonomy. The enlightened and high-minded Father Howard Kenna, the provincial superior of the Indiana Province of the Holy Cross Congregation from 1962 to 1970, working with Hesburgh, developed a plan to remove Notre Dame from the ownership of the Holy Cross community and transfer it to the Notre Dame Board of Trustees, enlarged and reorganized for the purpose. In 1967 this was done.

This historic change--commonplace among American private universities for nearly a century--made concrete the concept of academic freedom Hesburgh thinks so essential to a modern university. Of all the innumerable honors he has received, he most cherishes the Alexander Meiklejohn Award bestowed on him by the American Association of University Professors in 1970. In his response, Hesburgh repeated his exhortation to academic freedom, and added: "Each year brings a new crisis. When the battle seems newly won, hostilities break out on another front. Freedom will always be a problem. But, long live academic freedom."

The second change was the admission of women beginning in 1972. Hesburgh has long been that rare creature, a celibate cleric who loves, admires, and is at ease with women. "Where are the wives?" he used to inquire loudly, when the stags gathered on the old pattern. After a false start of trying to amalgamate with neighboring St. Mary's College for women, Notre Dame acted unilaterally. The change was not without problems, but nearly all concerned are happy with it. An all-male Notre Dame is inconceivable in the twenty-first century terms Hesburgh thinks of. The world has indeed two sexes. Ted Hesburgh knew it all along.

Practically all the Hesburgh accomplishments involve skill with words, and Hesburgh can be very good at that. He writes with uncommon ability, perhaps a heritage from his religious order, which has a long tradition of good English

prose. When he prepares, he is an excellent speaker; when he
doesn't, he often rambles. He is gifted with extraordinary
presence, and, as the many examples already quoted show,
sharp and telling repartee. Perhaps the best example of his
skill at turning things his way with a phrase occurred in the
spring of 1975 during a visit to the campus by President
Gerald Ford. The mostly student audience for Ford's honorary
degree was restive; some radical faculty had proposed a giant
walkout to express disapproval of Ford's Vietnam policy. As
the tension mounted, it came time for Hesburgh to introduce
Ford. He was brief, but his timing was perfect. "Mr.
President," he said, "I want you to meet the greatest student
body in the world." The place went wild. The tension was
lifted, the walkout, if any, was inconspicuous.

The Hesburgh appearance is a help in such situations.
Remarkably handsome in youth, he has retained his good looks
through greying hair and facial crinkles. Indeed, he is more
impressive as time goes on. Although of only average, or
less, height, his carriage is graceful. His dress is
severely clerical, but well-tailored and immaculate; he is
one of those people who looks dressed up even in a rowboat.

His physical appearance is a help to his steady poise.
He runs a meeting with dispatch, his benign smile easing the
hurt of those committee bores who want to prolong every
meeting into weariness. In one-on-one encounters he is
immensely effective: how and why are mysteries, for he is
not in the usual sense of the word charming. But he can talk
most people into doing what he wants; there is something
about him that makes one want to please him. He does not
inspire envy or jealousy. It is doubtful if he has many
enemies, always excepting the Notre Dame people who want to
capture him and can't, and the extremists on both sides of
the religious and social spectrums. For Hesburgh is above
all not extremist. One of his favorite phrases is "civil
discourse." Within that canon, he is the most tolerant of
administrators, the patron of the opposition. He was host to
two of the most controversial speeches of recent times:
Jimmy Carter's on U.S. foreign policy, and New York Governor
Mario Cuomo's on the Catholic public official and abortion.
He has encouraged discussion on both sides of just about

everything worthy of university-level discussion. This abstention from partisanship inspires, of course, few disciples. If Hesburgh has few enemies, he also has few intimates. He does not wear his heart on his sleeve, and rarely indulges in small talk beyond the usual civilities, which he does brilliantly. His memory for everything, especially names and faces, is phenomenal.

He is, in short, nearly an ideal public figure, and, like most ideals, lacking in the little human eccentricities and quirks that often endear idols to their public. He is compassionate, he is not amusing, he is not mercurial, he is obstinate, he is not mean, he is not intemperate, he is not avaricious. He is also not artistic. In an age of vulgarity he is never vulgar. He turns the same face to all, for he has only one. He is totally punctilious, answering every letter, noting every accomplishment, thanking every kindness. He is blessed with great good health, a free play of abundant energy, and sturdy independence. He is very manly.

Like his client students, he is a night owl. He loves the midnight hours, often working through them till dawn. He prefers mornings for sleep, saying his daily mass, which he has missed only once since ordination, preferably around noon. At Notre Dame he lives very simply, sleeping in a bare little room in the priests' residence hall, and taking with them his abstemious diet. He likes a Manhattan before dinner but rarely takes more than one, even on festive occasions. He reads constantly--history, biography, science, and lots of sci fi and mystery fiction. He is sui generis; one is hard put to think of anyone like him outside his own community. Inside it there are obvious parallels with Fathers Zahm, Burns, and Kenna, but he is not really like any of them.

Nor is he really like the man who has seized his imagination, the founder of Notre Dame, Father Edward Sorin. Hesburgh claims no kinship with Sorin, but he has a keen sense of history, and he often refers to the founder. His final address to the faculty was a minibiography of Sorin. While he did not draw them, there are some intriguing similarities. Both were possessed, even obsessed, with a vision of a great Notre Dame. Both were willful and obstinate in pursuit of their visions. Both wished to be

missionaries as young priests, and retained all their lives
something of the missionary spirit. Both were priests above
all. And both loved Notre Dame.

Sorin's shadow still hangs over Notre Dame, above all in
the place itself. The campus is uniquely beautiful, especially
the old parts that Sorin personally designed, whether he had
an architect or not. Much of it recalls Sorin's memories of
his native Sarthe Department in France, just north of the
valley of the Loire. But the spacing of the old buildings,
and the planting in the Main Quad, largely Sorin's work, are
superb. Few American colleges can rival its layout, none its
trees. Many besides Sorin and Hesburgh have loved the place,
but none has left a mark on it so powerful and so inimitable
as theirs.

Chronological Table, 1917–1989

1917
Theodore Martin Hesburgh born 25 May 1917 in Syracuse, New York, the second child and elder son of five children born to Theodore Bernard Hesburgh and Anne Marie (Murphy) Hesburgh.

1922-1930
Most Holy Rosary Grade School, Syracuse, New York.

1930-1934
Most Holy Rosary High School, Syracuse, New York.

1934-1937
University of Notre Dame, Notre Dame, Indiana.

1937-1940
Gregorian University, Rome, Italy, Ph.B.

1940-1943
Holy Cross College, Washington, D.C., S.T.L.

1943
Ordained to the priesthood, Congregation of Holy Cross, June 24, 1943.

1943-1944
Chaplain for the National Training School for Boys, Washington, D.C.

1943-1945
The Catholic University of America, Washington, D.C., S.T.D.

1945-1947   Chaplain to veterans, University of Notre Dame.

1945-1948   Instructor, Assistant Professor of Religion, University of Notre Dame.

1948-1949   Head, Department of Religion, University of Notre Dame.

1949-1952   Executive Vice-President, University of Notre Dame.

1952-1987   President, University of Notre Dame, succeeding Reverend John J. Cavanaugh, C.S.C.

1954-1966   Appointed member of the National Science Board, the first of fourteen presidential appointments.

1957-1972   Appointed by Eisenhower as a charter member of the United States Commission on Civil Rights.

1957-1970   Vatican City Permanent Representative, International Atomic Energy Agency.

1963-1970   President, International Federation of Catholic Universities.

1964   Awarded Medal of Freedom, the nation's highest civilian honor.

1967   Transfer of governance of Notre Dame to a predominantly lay Board of Trustees.

1969   Famous 15-minute "cease and desist" order during campus rebellion.

1969-1972   Chairman, United States Commission on Civil Rights.

1970   Meikeljohn Award for upholding academic
            freedom from American Association of
            University Professors

1971-1982   Chairman, Overseas Development Council.

1972   Established the Ecumenical Institute for
            Advanced Theological Studies, Tantur,
            Jerusalem, at the request of Pope Paul VI.

1972   Dismissed from Civil Rights Commission by
            Richard M. Nixon.

1972   Admission of women to undergraduate programs
            at Notre Dame.

1974-1975   Appointed to Presidential Clemency Board by
            Ford.

1977-1979   U.S. Ambassador and Chairman of the U.S.
            Delegation to the United Nations Conference on
            Science and Technology for Development, 1979,
            Vienna, Austria.

1979-1980   Co-Chairman of Cambodian Crisis Committee to
            avert mass starvation.

1979-1981   Chairman, U. S. Select Commission on
            Immigration and Refugee Policy.

1982   Appointed by Reagan as member of U.S. Official
            Observer Team for El Salvador Elections.

1983   Appointed by John Paul II to the Pontifical
            Institute for Culture.

1985   Established the Institute for International
            Peace Studies, University of Notre Dame,
            with the assistance of Joan Kroc.

1987   Retired as President of the University of
              Notre Dame.

1988-1989   Following a sabbatical year of travel, Father
              Hesburgh continues his work with the
              International Foundation for the Survival and
              Development of Humanity, Moscow. He remains
              active in a wide variety of projects for the
              advancement of world peace, nuclear disarmament,
              education, and development.

List of Abbreviations

C.S.C.   Congregatio a Sancta Cruce. Congregation of
                Holy Cross. Religious community to which
                Father Hesburgh belongs.

ERIC   Educational Resources Information Center
                Office of Educational Research and Improvement
                U.S. Department of Education
                Washington, D.C.

                Nationwide bibliographic database containing a
                wide variety of information sources in education.

GPO   United States Government Printing Office
                Washington, D.C.

OCLC   Online Computer Library Center
                Dublin, Ohio.

                Nationwide bibliographic database containing over
                18 million records.

SuDoc no.   Superintendent of Documents number used for some
                works issued by the United States Government
                Printing Office, Washington, D.C.

UDIS   Department of Public Relations and Information
                University of Notre Dame, Notre Dame, Indiana.

UNDA   The Archives of the University of Notre Dame
            607 Hesburgh Library, University of Notre Dame
            Notre Dame, Indiana.

            Official repository for Father Hesburgh's archival
            and manuscript collections.

Valentine   Number used to designate an item described in
no.   *Directory: Theodore M. Hesburgh Civil Rights
            Collection.* Compiled by William R. Valentine.
            Notre Dame, Ind.: Notre Dame Law School, Center
            for Civil Rights, 1976. Items listed in Valentine's
            Directory are available on microfilm in The
            Archives of the University of Notre Dame.

Archives and Manuscripts by
Wm. Kevin Cawley

Before Father Hesburgh began his thirty-five-year term as
president of the University of Notre Dame, he served as
executive vice-president (1949-1952). His office files from
these years contain correspondence, reports, articles of
administration, agenda, minutes, and publications. They
represent his work with the Academic Council, the Faculty
Board in Control of Athletics, the Building Committee, the
Board of Lay Trustees' Educational Affairs Committee, the
Laetare Medal Nominating Committee, the American Council on
Education, the Aspen Institute for Humanistic Studies, the
Ford Foundation's Fund for Adult Education, and the National
Education Association (5 linear feet).

As president of the University of Notre Dame from 1952
until 1987, Hesburgh maintained subject files (130 linear
feet) and correspondence files (135 linear feet). He also
saved personal papers documenting his activities outside the
university (175 linear feet).

Hesburgh's subject files, organized alphabetically and
then chronologically within each category, contain general
folders for each letter of the alphabet followed by folders
bearing more specific titles. The title of a folder sometimes
indicates the subject matter of the documents within,
sometimes names the organization, department, or individual
whose correspondence the folder contains. Most of these files
have to do with the business of the university, but a good
many concern outside activities. They consist chiefly of
letters received by Hesburgh and carbon copies of letters

sent by him, with occasional reports, memoranda, agenda, and invitations.

Hesburgh's correspondence files, arranged chronologically by year and alphabetically within each year, also contain letters received and carbons of letters sent. Ordinarily the correspondents represented here have not written as many letters as those who have their own folders among the subject files.

This series includes correspondence with Pope Pius XII, Pope Paul VI, Dwight D. Eisenhower, John F. Kennedy, Lyndon B. Johnson, Richard M. Nixon, Gerald Ford, Jimmy Carter, Ronald Reagan, and George Bush. But such a parade of famous names fails to indicate the scope of Hesburgh's correspondence. The list of correspondents for the first year of his presidency consists of 2123 different names; the list for 1963, ten years later, consists of 2421 different names. In volume his correspondence increased as years went on. The letters from 1953 take up three linear feet, those from 1963 four, those from 1973 five and a half, and those from 1983 six. The subject files contain a similar volume of correspondence for each year. Hesburgh kept in touch with cardinals, archbishops, bishops, and monsignors, with admirals, generals, and members of Congress, with scientists, philosophers, historians, and theologians. He personally responded to letters from ordinary people, answered their questions, dealt with their criticism, and helped solve their problems.

Hesburgh's personal papers, grouped according to the activity that generated them, contain some correspondence, but letters from people Hesburgh met through his activities outside the university also show up in his subject and correspondence files. The personal papers consist typically of material distributed to the members of boards of directors, committees, or commissions on which Hesburgh served, sometimes with his handwritten marginalia.

United States Commission on Civil Rights records (1958-1973) consist of reports, press releases, statements, resolutions, court material, correspondence, memoranda, proposals, minutes, agenda, pamphlets, clippings, transcripts of testimony given in hearings, and transcripts of speeches, press conferences, and broadcasts. They include letters from Richard M. Nixon and many others (40 linear feet).

National Science Foundation records (1954-1966) have to do with Hesburgh's service as a member of the National Science Board. They consist of agenda, minutes, memoranda, correspondence, reports, budgets, and lists of grants, fellowships and contracts awarded by the National Science Foundation (30 linear feet).

Rockefeller Foundation records (1962-1982) concern Hesburgh's work as trustee and chairman of the board (1977-1982) of the Rockefeller Foundation. They consist of dockets, agenda, minutes, correspondence, memoranda, proposals, and reports. They document activities of the Board of Trustees, the Executive Committee, and the Finance Committee, as well as foundation projects in international education and development, agriculture, health, and population control. They contain material on the John D. Rockefeller III Youth Award, and letters from John Knowles and George Harrar (20 linear feet).

International Atomic Energy Agency records (1956-1977) concern Hesburgh's work as Vatican delegate to the IAEA (1956-1971) and that of the other permanent delegate of the Vatican, American layman Frank M. Folsom. They consist of reports of the Vatican delegation with supporting documentation, agenda, proceedings of the General Conference of the IAEA and of its Board of Governors, letters from the Director General to the Vatican Secretary of State, information circulars, and press releases. They concern regulation of atomic energy and contain information on the United Nations Third International Conference on the Peaceful Uses of Atomic Energy (Geneva, 1964), to which Hesburgh was also a Vatican delegate (15 linear feet).

Carnegie Foundation records (1967-1976) have to do with Hesburgh's participation as a trustee of the Carnegie Foundation for the Advancement of Teaching and a member of the Carnegie Commission on Higher Education. They consist of agenda, minutes, correspondence, memoranda, and reports (10 linear feet of manuscripts and 10 linear feet of printed material, including the published reports of both the

Carnegie Commission on Higher Education and the Carnegie Council on Policy Studies in Higher Education).

National Cambodia Crisis Committee and *Cambodia Crisis Center* records (1979-1980) reflect Hesburgh's service as cochairman of the committee. They consist of correspondence, memoranda, circular letters, mailings, clippings, notes, brochures, and press releases. They concern efforts to disseminate information and raise funds to help Cambodia recover from famine, disease, and the devastation brought about by war and the reign of the Khmer Rouge. They include files on the corporate campaign, the AFL-CIO campaign, the state campaign, volunteer agencies, civic groups, the Ad Council, press, planning, and finances (10 linear feet).

Overseas Development Council records (1971-1982) have to do with Hesburgh's service as chairman of the Board of Directors. They consist of correspondence, memoranda, statements before congress, reports, agenda, and material from meetings of the Executive Committee and the Board of Directors. They concern relations between the United States and Third World countries, world hunger, the food crisis of 1974, and the citizens'-action group New Directions. They contain drafts and proofs of the Council's annual *Agenda for Action* and writings of James P. Grant, John W. Sewell, and Denis Goulet (5 linear feet).

International Federation of Catholic Universities records (1955-1978) represent Hesburgh's participation in efforts to clarify the relationship between modern Catholic universities and the Vatican, especially his work as president of the IFCU (1963-1970). They consist of Hesburgh's correspondence with the permanent secretariat of the IFCU in Paris, with other members of the federation, and with the Sacred Congregation for Catholic Education (Sacra Congregatio pro Institutione Catholica), reports, and other documents from meetings of the IFCU and of the congresses of delegates from Catholic universities convened by the Sacred Congregation for Catholic Education in Rome (1966 and 1972). They contain material from the two Land O'Lakes meetings (1967 and 1971) concerning the question of autonomy for Catholic universities and include correspondence with Hervé Carrier, S.J., Msgr. Georges

Leclercq, Cardinal Garrone, Neil G. McCluskey, and R. J. Henle, S.J. (5 linear feet).

Chase Manhattan Bank records (1972-1981) concern Hesburgh's service as a member of the Board of Directors and its Employee Benefits Review Committee. They consist of preliminary agenda for meetings of the board, correspondence, memoranda, reports, presentations, and financial papers and contain material on annual meetings of stockholders and on South African investment. They include correspondence with David Rockefeller (5 linear feet).

United States Advisory Commission for International Educational and Cultural Affairs records (1961-1965) consist of reports on the effectiveness of the educational and cultural exchange program of the U.S. Department of State; agenda, minutes, and study material of the commission; correspondence, memoranda, and press releases. They contain minutes of the Government Advisory Committee on International Book Programs and information on Fulbright scholars, the East-West Center in Honolulu, and American Studies abroad (3 linear feet).

Presidential Clemency Board records (1974-1975) consist of memoranda, handbooks, reports, agenda, minutes, press releases, essays on amnesty (1972-1974), and case summaries of individuals seeking pardon (3 linear feet).

United Nations Conference on Science and Technology for Development records (1977-1979) have to do with Hesburgh's service as United States Ambassador to the UNCSTD (Vienna, 1979). They consist of correspondence, memoranda, agenda, transcripts of meetings, statements, addresses, reports, national papers, proposals, plans, circulars, press releases, offprints, and clippings. They concern the work of the United States Delegation to the conference and include letters from Joel Bernstein, Ambassador Jean Wilkowski, and President Jimmy Carter (3 linear feet).

Midwest Universities Research Association records (1954-1968) consist of correspondence, memoranda, agenda, minutes, reports, contracts, bylaws, and proposals. They concern MURA's Board of Directors, individual members, Nominating Committee, Executive Committee, and treasurer. They contain records of the Policy Advisory Board of the Argonne National

Laboratory and documents on the Associated Midwest
Universities and have to do with the cooperative effort of
midwestern universities to support atomic energy research and
development (2 linear feet).

Institute of International Education records (1955-1973)
represent Hesburgh's work on the Board of Trustees. They
consist of agenda, minutes, reports, and correspondence. They
concern meetings of the board, the Conference on Higher
Education in the American Republics (CHEAR, 1965-1970), the
Fourth National Conference on Exchange of Persons
(*Educational Exchange for the Mutual Development of Nations*,
1960), the Fifth and Sixth Conferences on International
Education (1964 and 1969), the Advisory Committee of College
and University Presidents (1963), and the Ford International
Fellowship Advisory Board (1962-1964) (2 linear feet).

Peace Corps records (1961-1965) have to do with
Hesburgh's involvement with the Peace Corps of the United
States and one of its earliest projects, the training of
volunteers at Notre Dame for service in Chile. They consist
of correspondence, reports, newsletters, and course material.
They concern relations between universities and the Peace
Corps, Hesburgh's visits to Chile, the Chilean Christian
Housing Movement, and problems with cooperation of the Peace
Corps, the Indiana Conference of Higher Education, and
Chile's Institute of Rural Education. Correspondents include
Robert Sargent Shriver, Jr., Jaime Larrain, Jerome Judge,
and Peter Fraenkel (2 linear feet).

Institute for World Order records (1968-1982) have to do
with Hesburgh's participation in the World Order Models
Project of the World Law Fund, itself a project of the
Institute for International Order, later known as the
Institute for World Order. They represent an effort to
develop models of a future world order capable of sustaining
peace, social justice, economic welfare, and ecological
balance. They consist of agenda, minutes, correspondence,
financial statements, and reports. They concern the
Sponsoring and Policy Review Committee of the World Order
Models Project (1968-1972) and the Board of Directors of the
Institute (1972-1982) and contain photocopies of manuscripts
of *Preferred Worlds for the 1990s* by Saul H. Mendlovitz

(1973) and *A Study of Future Worlds* by Richard A. Falk (1974) along with material on the University Centers Program (1974), the Public Education Participation Program (Reassessing Values, Inc.), and conferences and seminars on world order (1974-1975) (2 linear feet).

Teachers' Insurance and Annuity Association of America and *The College Retirement Equities Fund* records (1975-1982) consist of agenda and correspondence concerning Hesburgh's participation (1975-present) as a trustee of TIAA stock and a member of CREF; minutes of meetings of TIAA Trustees, Executive Committee, Finance Committee, Mortgage Committee, and Audit Committee; minutes of meetings of CREF, its Board of Trustees, Executive Committee, Educator-Trustee Advisory Committee, and Finance Committee; and TIAA/CREF Quarterly Statistics and Audit Reports (2 linear feet).

Council on Foreign Relations records (1976-1982) concern Hesburgh's activity as a member and consist of agenda, minutes, correspondence, reports, and presentations. They contain information on proposed new members of the Board of Directors, the Nominating Committee, and the Membership Committee. They include letters from John Temple Swing and David Rockefeller (2 linear feet).

Select Commission on Immigration and Refugee Policy records (1980-1981) consist of reports, summaries of research, charts, and briefing papers used in meetings of SCIRP. They concern the proposed revision of the Immigration and Nationality Act and contain a copy of the commission's final report and recommendations, *U.S.Immigration Policy and the National Interest*, and related material on the Cuban / Haitian Task Force of the U.S. Department of Health and Human Services (2 linear feet).

Educational Services Incorporated records (1959-1967) consist of agenda, minutes, project fiscal reports, financial statements, current situation reports, and a proposal to the National Science Foundation. They concern meetings of members, trustees, and the Executive Committee and contain information on curricula developed by ESI (1 linear foot).

International Association of Universities records (1960-1975) consist of memoranda, reports, papers, agenda, lists of participants, and other material distributed at general meetings and at meetings of the administrative board (1 linear foot).

Select Committee on the Future of Private and Independent Education in New York State records (1967-1968) concern Hesburgh's work as a member of the Select Committee chaired by McGeorge Bundy. They consist of correspondence, memoranda, agenda, working papers, reports, and clippings regarding state support of private universities and colleges. Nelson Associates provided staff services for the committee, which studied reports gathered by Nelson and issued its own recommendations at the beginning of 1968 (1 linear foot).

President's Commission on an All-Volunteer Armed Force records (1969-1970) consist of correspondence, memoranda, agenda, minutes, position papers and reports (1 linear foot).

Commission on U.S.-Latin American Relations records (1974-1975) consist of agenda, minutes, discussion papers, and reports used in meetings of CUSLAR and include a copy of the commission's report (6 linear inches).

Potomac Institute Committee for the Study of National Service records (1977-1981) consist of correspondence, memoranda, minutes, reports, position papers, and clippings. They concern the idea that all Americans should dedicate a year of life to service. They include letters from Roger Landrum, Harris Wofford, and Jacqueline Grennon Wexler (6 linear inches).

Pan American Airlines International Advisory Board records (1977-1981) consist of agenda, memoranda, papers, reports, brochures, policy statements, and transcripts of talks documenting meetings of the board. They concern international air transport policy and the policies of Pan American Airlines and contain a commemorative booklet on the Iran Airlift (6 linear inches).

Hesburgh's personal papers also include records of his work with the National War College Board of Consultants (1967, 4 linear inches); the President's General Advisory Committee on Foreign Assistance Programs (1967-1968, 4 linear inches); the Committee of Americans for the Canal Treaties, Inc. (1972-1978, 2 linear inches); Project Cyclops and the Search for Extraterrestrial Intelligence (1975, 4 linear inches); the Advisory Board of People for the American Way (1980-1982, 4 linear inches); and other organizations.

The University Archives preserves Hesburgh photographs (5 linear feet), audio-visual material (3 linear feet), printed material (35 linear feet), unpublished addresses (3 linear feet), and artifacts such as the plaques and trophies associated with Hesburgh's awards and the robes and diplomas associated with his honorary degrees,

Ordinarily university records remain closed for fifty years after the date of their creation. In recognition of the unusual character of Father Hesburgh's files and in keeping with his wishes, the university's present administration has lifted this absolute restriction. Researchers interested in using Hesburgh's office files or personal papers should write to the University Archivist giving a precise description of their proposed research. The University Archivist will then review the pertinent files and determine whether the material they contain must remain confidential or if permission to use it may be granted.

Published Works:
Books by Theodore M. Hesburgh

1940-1949

1. *The Relation of the Sacramental Characters of Baptism
    and Confirmation to the Lay Apostolate.* The Catholic
    University of America. Studies in Sacred Theology,
    no. 97. Washington, D.C.: The Catholic University of
    America Press, 1946.

    Thesis (S.T.D.)--The Catholic University of America,
    1945.

2. *The Theology of Catholic Action.* Notre Dame, Ind.:
    University of Notre Dame, 1946.

    "The scope of this study is to determine the place
    and function of the layman in the Church, by a
    theological consideration of the basic structural
    sacraments of baptism and confirmation."--p. vii.

    Originally presented as a doctoral dissertation, The
    Catholic University of America, under the title *The
    Relation of the Sacramental Characters of Baptism and
    Confirmation to the Lay Apostolate.*

1950-1959

3.   *God and the World of Man*. University Religion
     Series. Texts in Theology for the Layman. Notre
     Dame, Ind.: University of Notre Dame Press, 1950.

     Textbook in religion which treats matters of faith,
     the knowledge and nature of God, the Holy Trinity,
     creation, original sin, and the end of the world.

     Second edition published in 1960.

4.   *Patterns for Educational Growth: Six Discourses
     at the University of Notre Dame*. Notre Dame, Ind.:
     University of Notre Dame Press, 1958.

     A series of six discourses originally delivered at
     the inaugural Mass at the beginning of each school
     year from 1952 to 1957. Includes "Wisdom and
     Education" (1952); "A Theology of History and
     Education" (1953); "The Mission of a Catholic
     University" (1954); "Education in a World of Social
     Challenge" (1955); "The Divine Element in Education"
     (1956); and "Education in a World of Science" (1957).

1960-1969

5.   *God and the World of Man*. 2d ed. University Religion
     Series. Theology for the Layman. Notre Dame, Ind.:
     University of Notre Dame Press, 1960.

     Hesburgh notes that many scientific and some theological
     developments have occurred regarding the origins of
     man and the world since his work was first published
     in 1950. In this edition, at Hesburgh's request,
     Rev. John Dunne, C.S.C., completely revised Chapter 5,
     Section 3: "How God Created," which deals with
     mythological cosmogony, scientific cosmogony, and
     evolution.

6.   *Thoughts for Our Times*. Thought Series, no. 1. Notre
     Dame, Ind.: University of Notre Dame, 1962.

     Three addresses: "Science and Technology in Modern
     Perspective" (Commencement address: Massachusetts
     Institute of Technology, 8 June 1962); "Science and
     Man" (delivered at a California Institute of
     Technology dinner honoring the National Science
     Board, Los Angeles, 16 November 1962); and "Change
     and the Changeless" (presented before the Winter
     Convocation of the University of Chicago, 15 December
     1961).

7.   *More Thoughts for Our Times*. Thought Series, no. 2.
     Notre Dame, Ind.: University of Notre Dame, 1964.

     Three addresses: "The Moral Dimensions of the Civil
     Rights Movement" (presented in November 1964, at a
     meeting of the American Academy of Arts and Sciences
     in Boston, Mass.); "The Cultural and Educational
     Aspects of Development" (address given at the annual
     International Conference of Pax Romana, July 1964,
     Washington, D.C.); and "The University in the
     World of Change" (delivered at the Fourth Annual
     Meeting of the Council of Graduate Schools, December
     1964, Chicago, Ill.).

8.   *Still More Thoughts for Our Times*. Thought Series,
     no. 3. Notre Dame, Ind.: Public Relations and
     Development, University of Notre Dame, 1966.

     Three addresses: "Our Revolutionary Age" (delivered
     at Commencement Exercises, University of Illinois,
     Urbana, Illinois, 18 June 1966); "The Forefront of
     Tomorrow's Knowledge" (delivered at the 16th Annual
     'University for Presidents' of the Young Presidents'
     Organization, Phoenix, Arizona, 25 April 1966); and
     "The Social Sciences in an Age of Social Revolution"
     (delivered at the dedication banquet of the Institute
     for Social Research, The University of Michigan, Ann

Arbor, 30 March 1966).

9.   *Thoughts IV: Five Addresses Delivered During 1967.*
Thought Series, no. 4. Notre Dame, Ind.: Public
Relations and Development, University of Notre Dame,
1967.

Primarily on the subject of education, these five
addresses include "The Vision of a Great Catholic
University in the World Today" (given at a Special
Convocation commemorating the 125th anniversary of
the founding of the University of Notre Dame,
9 December 1967); "The Challenge Ahead" (given at
the Annual Meeting of the Council of Protestant
Colleges and Universities, Los Angeles, 16 January
1967); "Service: The Great Modern Prayer" (given at
Commencement Exercises, Manchester College, North
Manchester, Indiana, 12 June 1967); "Year of Faith"
(sermon delivered in Sacred Heart Church, University
of Notre Dame, 5 November 1967, inaugurating a
series of sermons on the Year of Faith proclaimed by
Pope Paul VI); and "The Historical Evolution of the
Catholic View of Luther" (address given at
Valparaiso University Convocation, Valparaiso,
Indiana, 1 November 1967.)

Hesburgh considered the first talk, "The Vision of a
Great Catholic University in the World Today," among
the most important, since it is "a realistic blueprint
of what we hope to realize at Notre Dame, as a great
Catholic university, in the years ahead."--Foreword.

10.   *Thoughts for Our Time V.* Thought Series, no. 5.
Notre Dame, Ind.: President's Office, University of
Notre Dame, 1969.

Four addresses delivered during 1968 concerned with
two major categories: university education and human
rights. Includes "The Mission of the Catholic
University in the Modern World" (delivered 10 September

1968, at Lovanium University in Kinshasa, Congo
at the Eighth General Conference of the International
Federation of Catholic Universities); "In Defense of
the Younger Generation" (delivered 6 June 1968 at
Commencement Exercises, University of Southern
California, a few hours after the death of Senator
Robert Kennedy; "The Churches and the Struggle
Against Prejudice" (delivered 25 March 1968 at the
University of California, Berkeley, during a week-
long symposium on prejudice); and "On Human Rights"
(delivered at a United Nations conference in Teheran,
Iran, which Hesburgh attended as head of the Vatican
delegation).

1970-1979

11. Hesburgh, Theodore M., Paul A. Miller, and Clifton R.
    Wharton, Jr. *Patterns for Lifelong Learning*. The
    Jossey-Bass Series in Higher Education. San Fran-
    cisco: Jossey-Bass, 1973.

    Explores continuing education and the future,
    universities and the learning society, and the life-
    long university.

    ERIC ED 092 786.

12. *The Humane Imperative: A Challenge for the Year 2000*.
    The Terry Lectures. New Haven: Yale University
    Press, 1974.

    Hesburgh speculates on what the world will be like in
    the year 2000. He focuses on human dignity, human
    rights, human development, and justice. Theological
    and philosophical principles can become effective
    instruments of change in social, economic, political,
    educational, scientific, and technological areas.
    Upon these foundations, one can construct a better
    world, both human and divine.

13.   *Three Bicentennial Addresses.* Notre Dame, Ind.:
      Office of the President, University of Notre Dame,
      1976.

      Hesburgh prepared these three basic talks in 1976 on
      bicentennial themes which he used repeatedly on
      numerous occasions. Includes "Justice in America: The
      Dream and the Reality" delivered at the National
      Citizens' Assembly on Improving Courts and Justice,
      Philadelphia, 4 July 1976; "Religious Liberty in
      the International Scene" presented at the Bicenten-
      nial Conference on Religious Liberty, Philadelphia,
      29 April 1976; and "American Aspirations and the
      Grounds of Hope" delivered at the Notre Dame-Saint
      Mary's Bicentennial Conference, "An Almost Chosen
      People: The Moral Aspirations of Americans," 11 March
      1976.

14.   Hesburgh, Theodore M., and Louis J. Halle.
      *Foreign Policy & Morality: Framework for a Moral
      Audit.* New York: Council on Religion and
      International Affairs, 1979.

      Hesburgh and Halle approach foreign policy and morality
      from different points of view. Hesburgh's essay,
      "Moral Aspirations & American Foreign Policy" (pp. 10-
      26) discusses foreign policy from the standpoint of
      American responsibility to articulate its historic
      national goals and moral vision in foreign policy.
      Halle's essay, "Applying Morality to Foreign Policy"
      (pp. 27-37) favors not moral preachment, but moral
      example practiced primarily at home. Commentary
      and criticism, at times stringent, of both essays are
      offered by five representative thinkers: John C.
      Bennett, George F. Kennan, John P. Armstrong, Philip C.
      Jessup, and E. Raymond Platig.

      ERIC ED 194 443.

15. *The Hesburgh Papers: Higher Values in Higher Education.* Kansas City, Kans.: Andrews and McMeel, 1979.

In a series of eighteen essays, Hesburgh discusses values and leadership in Catholic and Christian higher education. He develops the idea of the formation of a great Catholic university in modern America, which he considers the central endeavor of his life. Chapters include "The Vision of the Catholic University in the World of Today"; "The Catholic University and Freedom"; "The Moral Purpose of Higher Education"; "In Defense of the Younger Generation"; "The Lessons of the Student Revolution"; and "Education in the Year 2000."

Includes two of Hesburgh's most influential letters, one addressed to Notre Dame faculty and students dated 17 February 1969 stating that "anyone or any group that substitutes force for rational persuasion, be it violent or non-violent, will be given fifteen minutes of meditation to cease and desist" (pp. 164-70), and Hesburgh's letter to Vice-President Spiro Agnew dated 27 February 1969, stating his views on campus unrest (pp. 170-73).

1980-1989

16. *O imperativo humanitário: um desafio para a ano 2000.* Trans. by Paulo Roberto Palm. Brasília: Editora Universidade de Brasília, 1980.

Originally delivered in English as the Dwight Harrington Terry Foundation Lecture on Religion in Light of Science and Philosophy. Portuguese translation of *The Humane Imperative: A Challenge for the Year 2000* (1974). No other translations of the work are available.

17. *Commitment, Compassion, Consecration: Inspirational Quotes of Theodore M. Hesburgh, C.S.C.* Selected and compiled by Thomas J. Mueller and Charlotte A. Ames. Huntington, Ind.: Our Sunday Visitor, 1989.

A brief biographical account and a selection of quotations from several of Hesburgh's addresses, essays, and published works.

Articles, Addresses, and Essays
by Theodore M. Hesburgh

1940-1949

18. "Election of Pius XII." *Ave Maria* 52 (10 August 1940): 175-76.

    From St. Peter's in Rome, Hesburgh describes the events which marked the election of Cardinal Pacelli as Pope Pius XII.

19. *Contact.* Washington, D.C.: National Catholic Community Service, 1945-   . UNDA: PMRH.

    Hesburgh joined Philip Wendell Shay in editing a series of pamphlets on faith and morals for Catholics in military service. G.I.s contributed their comments and concerns.

1950-1959

20. *Education for Responsible Leadership: An Address by the Rev. Theodore M. Hesburgh, C.S.C., President of the University of Notre Dame.* Notre Dame, Ind.: n.p., 1952. UDIS.

    Hesburgh describes values essential to the Christian formation of a good man: professional competence and moral responsibility.

21.   *Letters to Service Women.* Washington, D.C.: National
      Catholic Community Service, 1952.

      Hesburgh addresses a series of eight letters to Mary,
      Bets, and Anne, his sisters in military service. He
      points out the good and bad aspects of military life,
      and suggests practical spiritual tips for making the
      most of opportunities and overcoming difficulties.

22.   "University and Philosophy." American Catholic
      Philosophical Association. *Proceedings* 27 (1953):
      12-16.

      Hesburgh reflects on the role of the scientist, the
      theologian, and the philosopher in the university
      milieu. He envisions philosophers primarily as
      mediators, and encourages greater dialogue.

23.   "The True Spirit of Notre Dame." *Sports Illustrated*
      1 (27 September 1954): 16-20; 30-32.

      Hesburgh asserts that by applying the principle of
      considering the student's education first, major
      abuses in intercollegiate athletics could be
      eliminated. Includes four-page color portfolio with
      Irish quarterback Ralph Guglielmi and Notre Dame coach
      Terry Brennan.

24.   "Liberal Education in the World Today." *Association
      of American Colleges Bulletin* 41 (March 1955): 82-
      87.

25.   "Science and Modern Man: Address for the Dedication
      of Saint Mary's Science Hall, April 23, Holy Cross
      Day." *Chimes* 64, no. 4 (1955): 195-99.

      Hesburgh stresses the importance of integrating the
      knowledge of science with wisdom. The key problem

in education today is unity of knowledge.

26.   "Sex Education and Moral Values." In *Social Hygiene
       Papers: A Symposium on Sex Education*, edited by Edgar
       C. Cummings, 18-22. New York: American Social Hygiene
       Association, 1957.

       Hesburgh situates sex education in a Christian context,
       "interpreting sex in the light of a total consideration
       of man and his faculties; seeing sex education as a
       part of the total educational orientation of the human
       person; and viewing sexual morality as an integral part
       of a total system of moral values."--p. 18.

27.   "The Examined Life." *Dartmouth Alumni Magazine* (July
       1958): 16-19.

       Commencement address, Dartmouth College, 8 June 1958.
       Stresses the importance of individual identity and
       commitment to values.

                          1960-1969

28.   "Every Man Has a Right to Vote." *Catholic Digest*
       24 (August 1960): 27-31.

29.   "A Universal Suffrage Law." *Interracial Review* 33
       (July 1960): 178-79.

       Hesburgh discusses efforts of the Civil Rights
       Commission to ensure the right to vote for the
       disenfranchised, particularly blacks in the South.
       He probes the question of literacy as a qualification
       for voting the the United States. Excerpts from
       Hesburgh's address at the Notre Dame Law School
       Conference on Civil Rights held in February.
       Reprinted from the *Catholic Messenger*.

30. "What Should U.S. Do About World Population
    Problem?" *Foreign Policy Bulletin* 39 (15 May 1960):
    132, 134.

    Hesburgh observes that the population problem can be
    considered a crisis or an opportunity. He discusses
    the Catholic position on artificial birth control.
    As a matter of policy, he suggests that we offer
    assistance to underdeveloped areas by helping them to
    raise food production and distribution, hasten
    economic growth, and increase educational and cultural
    opportunity.

31. "Catholic Higher Education in Twentieth-Century
    America." *Scholastic* 102 (21 April 1961): 15-17.

    Address given at the National Catholic Educational
    Association, April 1961. Preservation of unchanging
    values and adaptation to dynamic change are required
    for Catholic education to become a vital and vigorous
    force in our time. The essential task facing
    Catholic higher education is mediation. Also published
    in *Notre Dame Alumnus*, vol. 38, June 1961, pp. 3-5;
    and *National Catholic Educational Association Bulletin*
    vol. 58, August 1961, pp. 90-103.

32. "Catholics and the Present." *Commonweal* 74 (12 May
    1961): 178-79.

    Excerpts from "Catholic Higher Education in Twentieth
    Century America."

33. "Education for Citizenship." In *The Challenge to
    American Education* by the Anti-Defamation League of
    B'nai B'rith, 8-11. New York: Anti-Defamation League
    of B'nai B'rith, 1961. UNDA: UDIS-Biographical Files.

    Address delivered at the Freedom Forum, 14 January
    1961, Temple Emanu-El, New York City. Love of truth
    and beauty, a passion for justice, and compassion for

those less fortunate than ourselves constitute the
basic values of education.

34.   "Report on Civil Rights." *Scholastic* 103 (15 December
1961): 24-26.

Contains text of Hesburgh's statement appended to the
second report of the United States Commission on
Civil Rights.

35.   Review of *Atomic Energy and Law: Interamerican
Symposium,* edited by Jaro Mayda. *Notre Dame
Lawyer* 37, no. 1 (Symposium, 1961): 117-18.

Hesburgh's book review provides a comprehensive summary
of the record of an Interamerican Symposium held in San
Juan, Puerto Rico, 16-19 November 1959 on the legal and
administrative implications of peaceful atomic energy
programs.

36.   "The Work of Mediation." *Commonweal* 75 (6 October
1961): 33-35.

Hesburgh discusses mediation in the context of the
priesthood of Christ, the work of redemption, and the
mission of Catholic universities to preserve their
heritage of theological wisdom.

37.   "Looking Back at Newman." *America* 106 (3 March
1962): 720-21.

Compares the world today with the world in which John
Henry Newman wrote. The mission of the Catholic
university is redemptive.

38.   "Modern Perspective on Faith and Secular Knowledge."
World Campus (December 1962): 4. UNDA.

Valentine no. 5552.

39. "Science and Technology in Modern Perspective." *Vital Speeches* 28 (1 August 1962): 631-34.

Discusses science and technology, as forms of knowledge and power, in relation to human values of truth, excellence, justice, and faith.

40. "Science and Man: People Are Coming out Second Best to Things." *Vital Speeches* 29 (1 January 1963): 174-77.

The nature and destiny of man are essentially philosophical and theological questions rather than scientific or technological questions.

41. "Science Is Amoral: Need Scientists Be Amoral, Too?" *Saturday Review* 46 (2 March 1963): 55-56.

Hesburgh suggests that it might be appropriate for scientists and engineers to become philosophers and theologians in order to question the moral impact of their work on the world in which they live. Also published in *Way* (U.S.), vol. 19, April 1963, pp. 20-25.

42. "This New Generation: An Appraisal." *America* 109 (5 October 1963): 383-84.

Hesburgh endorses *New Generation*, a journal of student opinion which began in 1963, edited by Catholic students in both Catholic and secular colleges. "What especially recommends this publication is that it is not tied to any one particular institution and therefore is not saddled with institutional responsibility or representation."--p. 384.

43. "Thoughts For Graduates in 1963." *Way* (U.S.) 19 (June 1963): 29-31.

44.   "The Cultural and Educational Aspects of Develop-
ment." Address delivered at the Biennial Interfederal
Assembly of PAX ROMANA, Georgetown University,
Washington, D.C., 21 July 1964. Monographics 1.
Paris: International Federation of Catholic
Universities, 1964. 23 pp. UNDA: PPHS.

Hesburgh demonstrates that people in Catholic
universities possess the means essential to any
adequate solution to the total problem of human
development. Planning for development must begin with
a profound understanding of historical, cultural,
social, economic, political, and geographical facts.
Includes summaries in French and Spanish. An excerpt of
this address was published as "The Challenge of Under-
development," *Catholic Mind,* vol. 62, November 1964,
pp. 9-15.

45.   "On Being Number One." *Scholastic* 106 (4 December
1964): 13.

Text of an article written 28 November 1964 on
becoming number one. Spirit "has a kinship with the
spiritual in sport." Good sportsmanship implies
maturity.

46.   "Prevailing Winds on the Catholic Campus." *Critic* 22
(January 1964): 58-59.

With six other authorities familiar with Catholic
education, Hesburgh responds to the question: "What
evidence of 'the fresh wind blowing through the Church'
do you see in Catholic colleges and universities in
America?" Hesburgh welcomes increased lay activity in
the Church, and predicts it will become even more
significant in the future.

47.   "Cultural and Educational Development." *Catholic
Business Education Review* 16 (Summer 1965): 46-47.

48.   "College Football: The True Meaning of the Game."
      Sports Illustrated 25 (12 December 1966): 56-57.

      Hesburgh situates college football in the broader
      context of learning, education, and life.

49.   "The University in the World of Change." *Catholic
      Business Education Review* 17 (Summer 1966): 36-45.

      Discusses processes of human emancipation, human
      development, and technological innovation in the
      context of the mission of the university.

50.   "Dedication: Dean Joseph O'Meara." *Notre Dame
      Lawyer* 42 (Symposium, 1967): 854.

      Hesburgh pays tribute to Joseph O'Meara, dean of the
      Notre Dame Law School from 1952 to 1967, on the
      occasion of O'Meara's resignation.

51.   "Our Revolutionary Age." *Catholic Business Education
      Review* 18 (Spring 1967): 8-16.

      Hesburgh examines the processes of change, and
      recommends the values of commitment, compassion, and
      consecration as three essential ingredients of a
      meaningful life.

52.   "Preparing the Total Person." *Ave Maria* 105 (11
      February 1967): 10-11.

      Hesburgh discusses the knowledge explosion and the
      potential of worldwide telecommunication networks to
      expand the horizens of teaching and knowledge. The
      man of tomorrow will need wisdom and humanism as
      never before.

53.   "Science and Man." *Catholic Business Education Review*
      19 (Winter 1967): 6-12.

54.   "The Social Sciences in an Age of Social Revolution."
      Catholic Business Education Review 18 (Summer 1967):
      18-26.

55.   "Change and the Changeless." *Catholic Business
      Education Review* 20 (Winter 1968): 6-11.

56.   "Compassion Means Involvement." *Providence* 5 (Fall
      1968): 4-7.

      Commencement Address, Providence College, Providence,
      Rhode Island, 4 June 1968. Hesburgh urges educated
      Christians to "cultivate compassion in their inmost
      hearts and begin to weigh the contribution of human
      love that they can make to the world."--p. 7.

57.   "Freedom." In *Awake Throughout the Land,* by Kenneth
      D. Wells and Ruth E. Wells. Valley Forge, Pa.:
      Kenneth B. Wells, 1968.

      In a small unpaged volume, Hesburgh contributes a
      letter in which he defines freedom. "Freedom is what
      men live for and die for. It is both a condition and
      a state, a condition of life for men who understand
      human dignity and want to realize all its best
      potentialities; a state of the human existence that
      makes possible all good and all evil."

58.   "Scientists Cannot Be Neutral." *Scientific Research* 3
      (August 19, 1968): 40-46. UDIS.

      "The point I want to make is that the beginning of
      significant human leadership involves deep respect
      for the totality of man's intellectual and moral
      heritage and active cultivation of wide areas of
      wisdom above and beyond science and technology."
      --pp. 45-46.

59.   "The Vision of a Great Catholic University in the
      World of Today." In *The University in a Developing*

World Society: A Commemorative Volume Presented by The University of Notre Dame, 63-85. Notre Dame, Ind.: University of Notre Dame, 1968.

Symposium commemorating the 125th Anniversary Celebration of the University of Notre Dame: 1842-1967. Reprinted in *Notre Dame Journal of Education*, vol. 4, Fall 1973, pp. 228-38.

60.   "Action in the Face of Student Violence." *Catholic Mind* 67 (April 1969): 13-19.

Text of Hesburgh's letter of 17 February 1969 to faculty members, students and their parents on the subject of violent student demonstrations, followed by his letter of 25 February 1969 to Vice-President Spiro Agnew on the same subject. Also published in *Priest*, vol. 25, April 1969, pp. 231-36. Excerpts of Hesburgh's letter to faculty and students published under title "Dealing With Campus Chaos: Notre Dame: 15 Minutes and Out" in *U.S. News and World Report*, vol. 66, March 3, 1969, p. 34. Excerpts of his letter to Agnew published under title "Father Hesburgh: 'Crisis Will Pass.'" in *U.S. News and World Report*, vol. 66, March 10, 1969, p. 11.

61.   "The Changing Face of Catholic Higher Education." *National Catholic Educational Association Bulletin* 66 (August 1969): 54-60.

Hesburgh discusses three main foci for providing changes in Catholic higher education: trustees, faculty, and students. Address given at the 66th Annual Convention of the National Catholic Educational Association, Detroit, 8 April 1969.

62.   "A College President Takes a Stand on Campus Chaos." *Reader's Digest* 94 (May 1969): 104-7.

"After notification of suspension, or trespass in the case of non-community members, if there is not within five minutes a movement to cease and desist, students will be notified of expulsion from this community and the law will deal with them as non-students."--p. 105. Condensed from Hesburgh's Open Letter.

63. "Commencement Address Given at St. Louis University, St. Louis, Missouri, May 31, 1969." *College and University Development* 1 (Winter 1969): 8-11. UDIS.

Offers four-point national program for youth.

64. "Good Teachers, Good Schools." *Catholic School Journal* 69 (September 1969): 42.

65. "The Moral Basis of Personal Commitment." *Notre Dame Lawyer* 44 (1969): 1082-88.

Hesburgh states as his theme the future of the Notre Dame Law School. He portrays in detail the life of St. Thomas More "who carried the mind and heart of Christ from the courts of the poor to the palaces of kings, who so cherished the ideals of human law and human justice under God that he gladly gave his life rather than betray them."--p. 1088. Address given 8 February 1969, at the close of the Notre Dame Law School Centennial.

66. "A National Service Proposal." *Phi Delta Kappan* 51 (September 1969): 29-31.

67. "Opening Address." In *The Catholic University in the Modern World,* by the International Federation of Catholic Universities, 19-28. Paris: Secrétariat Permanent de la F.I.U.C., 1969.

1970-1979

68. Appendix. In *Student Activism and Higher Education:
     An Inter-American Dialogue*, by the Council on Higher
     Education in the American Republics. New York:
     Council on Higher Education in the American
     Republics, 1970.

69. Commentary. In *Recent Alumni and Higher Education: A
     Survey of College Graduates*, by Joe L. Spaeth and
     Andrew M. Greeley, 187-196. New York: McGraw Hill,
     1970.

     Hesburgh responds to the conclusions of this sociologi-
     cal and statistical study, indicating that unexplored
     territory reamins to be covered in further studies of
     the Carnegie Commission on Higher Education.

70. "Reform and the Future of the American Catholic
     University." In *University Reform: U.S.A., 1970: A
     Symposium on the Occasion of the Inauguration of
     Robert J. Henle, S.J. as 45th President of
     Georgetown University, October 7, 1969*, 1-11.
     Washington, D.C.: Georgetown University Press, 1970.

     Hesburgh discusses the specific role of the Catholic
     university in the world of universities; the acceptance
     of its importance by Catholics and others; greater
     support while preserving freedom and autonomy; and
     the dedication of many individuals in religious commun-
     ities who gave birth to Catholic universities.

71. "The 12th Alexander Meiklejohn Award." *AAUP Bulletin*
     56 (March 1970): 148-52.

     Includes Meiklejohn Award citation and Hesburgh's
     acceptance speech in which he enunciates principles
     of academic freedom.

72. "Catholic Education and the Challenge of the Seventies." *Notre Dame Journal of Education* 2 (Spring 1971): 5-12.

    Address given at the 68th Annual Convention of the National Catholic Educational Association, Minneapolis, Minn., 12 April 1971.

73. "The Challenge to Education." *Journal of Negro Education* 40 (Summer 1971): 290-96.

74. "Closing Remarks: Reflections of a President." In *The Task of Universities in a Changing World*, edited by Stephen D. Kertesz, 489-94. International Studies of the Committee on International Relations, University of Notre Dame. Notre Dame, Ind.: University of Notre Dame Press, 1971.

75. "A Crisis of Vision." Editorial. *Kiwanis* 56 (February 1971): 17. UNDA: UDIS-Biographical Files.

76. "Higher Education Begins the Seventies." In *Representative American Speeches: 1970-1971*, edited by Waldo W. Braden, 85-93. The Reference Shelf, v. 43, no. 4. New York: H. W. Wilson, 1971.

77. "Integer Vitae: Independence of the United States Commission on Civil Rights." *Notre Dame Lawyer* 46 (1971): 445-60.

    An essay on the early history of the United States Commission on Civil Rights.

78. "Mr. Secretary: Please Reconsider; Letter to George Romney." *America* 124 (6 March 1971): 238-39.

79. "The Nature of the Challenge: Traditional Organization and Attitudes of Universities Toward Contemporary Realities." In *The Task of Universities in a Changing World*, edited by Stephen D. Kertesz,

3-11. International Studies of the Committee on
International Relations, University of Notre Dame.
Notre Dame, Ind.: University of Notre Dame Press,
1971.

80.   "Resurrection for Higher Education." *Notre Dame
Report* 1 (1971): 56-61.

Text of a keynote address delivered at the 54th annual
meeting of the American Council on Education, 7 October
1971 in Washington, D.C.. Also published in *Educational Record*, vol. 53, Winter 1972, pp. 5-11. Excerpt
published under title "Presidential Leadership" in
Journal of Higher Education, vol. 42, December 1971,
pp. 763-65.

81.   "Barrier to Brotherhood." *Origins* 1 (16 March 1972):
652ff.

Testimony on busing.

82.   "The Commission on Civil Rights--and Human Rights."
Review of Politics 34 (July 1972): 291-305.

From his vantage point of serving 14 years on the
Civil Rights Commission, Hesburgh presents a seasoned
critique of the Commission, commenting on its
history, its structure, its frustrations, and its
accomplishments.

83.   "The Contemporary Catholic University: A Report."
Notre Dame Magazine 1 (April 1972): 14-46.

Excerpts from a position paper prepared by the North
American section of the International Federation of
Catholic Universities. Hesburgh participated
prominently in discussions which covered university
autonomy, the university and society, academic
dialogue, pastoral concerns, and world development.

84. Introductory Remarks. Notre Dame Law School Civil Rights Lectures. *Notre Dame Lawyer* 48 (1972): 6-11.

85. "The Last Word." *Notre Dame Magazine* 1 (December 1972): 31.

    Hesburgh joins several members of the university community in composing his own epitaph.

86. "1972 Laetare Medal." *Notre Dame Report* 1 (1972): 192.

    Hesburgh comments on the life and work of Dorothy Day, recipient of the 1972 Laetare Medal, the University's highest honor.

87. "Toward Racial Justice: A Call for Massive Change." *Current* 146 (December 1972): 3-13.

    Article based on Hesburgh's speech at Union Theological Seminary upon receiving the Reinhold Niebuhr Award.

88. "Tribute to Eli Ginzberg." In *Human Resources and Economic Welfare: Essays in Honor of Eli Ginzberg,* edited by Ivar Berg, 341-54. New York: Columbia University Press, 1972.

89. "Eulogy for I. A. O'Shaughnessy." *Notre Dame Report* 3 (1973): 200-203.

    Hesburgh renders final tribute to Ignatius Aloysius O'Shaughnessy, one of the University's most generous benefactors.

90. "Ite, Missa Est." In *Rev. Howard J. Kenna, C.S.C., 1901-1973,* 3-6. Notre Dame, Ind.: University of Notre Dame, 1973. UNDA: UDIS-Biographical Files.

Eulogy for Rev. Howard J. Kenna, C.S.C., who served
as Provincial, Indiana Province, Congregation of the
Holy Cross from 1962 to 1973. Hesburgh commends Doc,
"The Great Stone Face," for holding the community
together during difficult times.

91.   "A New Vision for Spaceship Earth." *Notre Dame Report*
2 (1973): 446-50.

"A new global vision is needed if man is to create on
earth the beauty that this planet manifests and seems
to promise from afar. The vision must be one of social
justice, of the interdependence of all mankind on this
small spacecraft. Unless the equality, and the one-
ness, and the common dignity of mankind pervade the
vision--the only future of this planet is violence and
destruction on an ever increasing scale, a crescendo of
man's inhumanity to man that can only result globally
in the extermination of mankind by man."--p. 447.
Harvard University Commencement Address, Harvard
University, Cambridge, Massachusetts, 13 June 1973.
Also issued separately as a booklet by the Department
of Public Relations and Information, University of
Notre Dame, 1973.

92.   "What Can We Do To Overcome Unnecessary Polarizations
in the Church?" In *Polarization in the Church*, edited
by Hans Küng and Walter Kaspar, 131-32. Concilium:
Religion in the Seventies, vol. 88. New York: Herder
and Herder, 1973.

Hesburgh observes that polarized Christians will
always be with us since the Church as a living body
is concerned with burning questions of salvation,
faith, values and eternity. He suggests five points
to help overcome unproductive polarization.

93.   "What Chance Does Peace Have?" *Origins* 2 (22 February
1973): 549ff.

Complete text of the 28 January 1973 campus observance marking the Vietnam cease-fire.

94. "Achieving Civil Rights." *Current* 167 (November 1974): 11-18.

95. "Amnesty--A Dirty Word?" *Notre Dame Magazine* 3 (October 1974): 15.

   Hesburgh discusses the moral dilemma of the Vietnam war, bombings in Cambodia, and his position favoring unconditional amnesty.

96. "Best and the Brightest." *Newsweek* 84 (22 July 1974): 11.

   Hesburgh suggests that a presidential candidate, "*in order to be elected*--let us know the kind of people he desires and *can indeed enlist* to share the momentous task that will await him . . . ."

97. "Civil Rights: Old Victories, New Battles." *Nation* 219 (14 September 1974): 207-10.

98. "The 'Events': A Retrospective View." *Daedalus* 103 (Fall 1974): 67-71.

99. "If You Were Truly Brothers." *Saint Luke's Journal of Theology* 18 (December 1974): 38-51.

   Discusses the problems and opportunities of an interdependent planet. Founder's Day Address, The University of the South, 10 October 1974.

100. "A Rapidly Changing Catholicism." *Notre Dame Magazine* 3 (June 1974): 21 ff.

   Hesburgh compares and contrasts changes in the Church since Vatican II. He envisions one Christian Church in the future, characterized by unity, but not

uniformity. Address to the joint national convention
of the Catholic Press Association and the Associated
Church Press, Denver, 24 April 1974.

101. "Toward More Food Aid." *Origins* 4 (12 December 1974):
392-93.

Text of a letter released 22 November 1974 at a
Washington, D.C., press conference appealing to
President Gerald Ford for an additional four million
tons of American food for the starving world.

102. "What Ever Happened to the Good Life?" *AAUW Journal*
(April 1974): 2.

Discusses the quality of life and those values which
give life meaning. All educators must become more
value conscious in order to avoid producing morally
illiterate graduates.

103. "Will There Still Be a God?" *Saturday Review World* 1
(24 August 1974): 82ff.

Hesburgh contends that whatever changes transpire
within the next fifty years, we "will still need faith
in God, and in His Providence, if this world of ours
is not to become a vast insane asylum."--p. 89.
Condensed version published under title "Why Believe
in God?" in *Catholic Digest*, vol. 39, January 1975,
pp. 22-25.

104. "Development: For Whom and For What." In *The
Participation of Catholic Universities in Research and
Education in the Fields of Population and Human
Development*, by the International Federation of Cath-
olic Universities, 49-61. Paris: I.F.C.U. Permanent
Secretariate, 1975.

In his report to the 11th General Assembly of the
International Federation of Catholic Universities,

New Delhi, 14-17 August 1975, Hesburgh evaluates past and present development policies, and advocates integral human development for all people of all nations as a prerequisite for lasting peace.

105. "Father Hesburgh's Eulogy for Richard Tucker, Saint Patrick's Cathedral, Oct. 14, 1975." *Notre Dame Report* 5 (1975): 137-39.

Hesburgh pays lasting tribute to the memory of Richard Tucker, one of America's greatest tenors who touched the nation with his spirit and his voice.

106. "Food in an Interdependent World." *Notre Dame Magazine* 4 (April 1975): 22-27.

Hesburgh focuses on the global food problem.

107. "Legislative Attitudes." In American Council on Education. *Education and State*, edited by John F. Hughes, 246-51. Washington, D.C.: American Council on Education, 1975.

108. "The Message of Brown for White America." In *The Continuing Challenge: The Past and the Future of Brown v. Board of Education. A Symposium*, 81-85. Evanston, Ill.: Published for Notre Dame Center for Civil Rights, Notre Dame, Indiana, by Integrated Education Associates, 1975.

ERIC ED 111 064.

109. "The Problems and Opportunities on a Very Inter-dependent Planet." *Ditchley Journal* (Spring 1975): 17-31.

The Ditchley Foundation Lecture delivered at Ditchley Park, Oxfordshire, England, 20 September 1974. Hesburgh develops his theme of interdependence using the food crisis and the population problems in the

countries of the Fourth World: India, China, Bangla-
desh, Indonesia, and Pakistan.

110. "They Found Sanctity Through Their Life Together."
      Agape (August 1975): 8-9. UDIS.

      Illuminates the spirituality of the laity as exemplified
      in the lives of Pat and Patty Crowley, founders of
      the Christian Family Movement.

111. "What Were Your Hopes for, and Vision of the Church
      in 1961?" *Critic* 34 (Fall 1975): 14-23.

      With John Tracy Ellis, Patricia Crowley, Kenneth
      Woodward, and others, Hesburgh expresssed his hopes
      for the Church before Vatican II. "I especially
      hoped for a greater Christian concern for world
      problems of justice, a vernacular liturgy, a de-
      triumphalized Christ, greater dependence on the
      inspiration and inner leadership of the Holy Spirit."
      --p. 23.

112. "American Aspirations and the Grounds of Hope." In *An
      Almost Chosen People: the Moral Aspirations of
      Americans*, edited by Ronald Weber and Walter
      Nicgorski, 131-46. Notre Dame, Ind.: University of
      Notre Dame Press, 1976.

      Hesburgh traces the history of political development
      in the United States, beginning with colonial times
      and the arrival of the British in Virginia and the
      Pilgrims in New England. Originally delivered at a
      Bicentennial conference held at the University of
      Notre Dame in 1976. Also published in *Review of
      Politics*, vol. 38, July 1976, pp. 423-38.

113. "Growing up Catholic in America: Ten Americans
      Reflect on Their Catholic Upbringing and What it
      Means to Them Today." *St. Anthony Messenger* 83
      (January 1976): 22-34.

114. "Guess Who's for the ERA?" *Ms* 4 (January 1976): 60.

    Comments shared with Carol Kleiman, *Chicago Tribune.*

115. Coles, Robert, Theodore M. Hesburgh, and Herbert
    Scoville. "That Person Should Be the Next President
    Who---." *Worldview* 19 (January-February 1976): 4-6.

116. "The American Responsibility for Fostering Religious
    Liberty Internationally." *Journal of Ecumenical
    Studies* 14 (Fall 1977): 135 (703)-145 (713).

    Focuses on religious liberty established in America.

117. "And They Called It the University of Notre Dame du
    Lac." *Notre Dame Magazine* 6 (April 1977): 10-18.

    Hesburgh profiles the history of Notre Dame and the
    need for greater resources in order to achieve Sorin's
    vision of a great Catholic university.

118. "The Carter Expedition." *Chief Executive* 1 (July,
    August, September 1977): 34-35. UDIS.

    In a rare piece of creative writing, Hesburgh pens
    the imaginary travels of President Jimmy Carter's
    grandson to another planet. He probes the require-
    ments for survival of a truly human life.

119. "Disciplines Enriched." *Journal of Teacher Education*
    28 (1977): 55.

120. "Father Hesburgh's Eulogy for George Shuster, Sacred
    Heart Church, Jan. 28, 1977." *Notre Dame Report* 6
    (1977): 278-80.

    Prior to his death on 25 January 1977 George
    Shuster, formerly president of Hunter College (1940-
    1960), served as Hesburgh's special assistant. "He
    engendered faith and hope and love because he lived

to the fullest these great virtues that lead us to
God."--p. 280.

121. "Father Ned Joyce: Filling the Bill." *Notre Dame
Magazine* 6 (June 1977): 24-25.

Hesburgh pays warm tribute to his closest associate,
Rev. Edmund P. Joyce, C.S.C., executive vice-
president of Notre Dame since 1952, after 25 years of
service.

122. "Justice in America: The Dream and the Reality."
Wisconsin Bar Bulletin 50 (1977): 17-21.

Hesburgh draws on colonial history, the Declaration
of Independence, and the Constitution as he examines
religious liberty, human dignity, and human rights.
Presented at the National Citizens' Assembly on
Improving Courts and Justice on 4 July 1976 in
Philadelphia.

123. "Letter to President Carter on Bakke Case." *Notre
Dame Report* 7 (October 18, 1977): 154-55.

Hesburgh's letter refers to *Regents of the University
of California v. Allan Bakke.* He offers several
principles which must be maintained in order to avoid
educational regression.

124. "Making Prophecies of Our Goals." In *The Third
Century: Twenty-Six Prominent Americans Speculate on
the Educational Future*, 188-91. New Rochelle, N.Y.:
Change Magazine Press, 1977.

125. "Should We Be Less Idealistic?" *Notre Dame Magazine* 6
(October 1977): 17.

Hesburgh recalls his debate with the Soviets in June
1977, and his recommendation for a U.S.-Soviet
student exchange. He states that criticism is

justified when the Soviets act in gross violation of
the International Declaration of Human Rights.

126. "The Presidency: A Personalistic Manifesto." In
Leadership for Higher Education: The Campus View,
edited by Roger W. Heyns, 1-11. Washington, D.C.:
American Council on Education, 1977.

Hesburgh outlines characteristics of effective
presidential leadership. Paper presented at the 59th
annual meeting of the American Council on Education,
New Orleans, 6-8 October 1976. Reprinted in *The
Hesburgh Papers* (1979), pp. 2-16.

127. *La Universidad Católica en el mundo de hoy.* Coleccion
"Documentos." Santiago de los Caballeros, República
Dominicana: Universidad Católica Madre y Maestra,
1977.

"The Catholic University in the World Today," an
address delivered at a breakfast sponsored by the
daily newspaper *Ultima Hora.*

128. "Worlds Apart: U.S. and Soviet Ideas About Freedom."
Civil Liberties Review 4 (September-October 1977):
46-52.

Highlights of a U.S.-Soviet debate moderated by Edwin
Newman, broadcast live on NBC TV, Sunday, 12 June
1977 at Georgetown University. Hesburgh, Robert G.
Kaiser of the *Washington Post,* and Alan M. Dershowitz
of Harvard Law School represented the United States.
Representing the Soviets were Samuel Zivs of the
Soviet Academy of Sciences; Ghenrih Borovik,
playwright and journalist; and August Mishin of the
Faculty of Law, Moscow University. Hesburgh stresses
the need for mutual understanding as crucial for
peaceful relations, and suggests a student exchange
program as a pathway to peace. Transcript of the
entire debate was issued as *Human Rights: A Soviet-*

American Debate. Washington, D.C.: Radio TV
Reports, 1977.

129. "Civil Rights and the Woman's Movement." In *The
Higher Education of Women: Essays in Honor of
Rosemary Park,* edited by Helen S. Astin and Werner Z.
Hirsh, 172-80. New York: Praeger, 1978.

ERIC ED 156 089.

130. "A Feast of Children." *Notre Dame Magazine* 7
(December 1978): 48.

Hesburgh reflects on Christmas as the quintessential
feast of children--a feast of divine love.

131. "Forgiving." In *The Ann Landers Encyclopedia, A to Z:
Improve Your Life Emotionally, Medically, Sexually,
Socially, Spiritually,* 467-68. Garden City: Double-
day, 1978.

Hesburgh explains forgiveness in the context of the
Prodigal Son and the Lord's Prayer. He suggests that
we should all be forgiving and merciful without measure
since we all are in need of mercy and forgiveness
ourselves.

132. "Is Solzhenitsyn Right?" *Time* 111 (26 June 1978):
18.

Hesburgh responds to Solzhenitsyn's Harvard address
which chided U.S. absorption with the comfortable
life.

133. "A New Vision for the Year 2000." In "Discours de
rentrée prononcé à l'ouverture de l'année
académique 1978-1979" by Édouard Massaux, 16-21.
Louvain-la-Neuve: Université Catholique de Louvain,
1978. UNDA.

Hesburgh considers the condition of one billion people in the Fourth World, largely illiterate, who consequently live in lifelong darkness.

134. "The Problems and Opportunities on a Very Interdependent Planet." In *Go Forth, Be Strong: Advice and Reflections From Commencement Speakers,* edited by Francis H. Horn, 142-56. Carbondale: Southern Illinois University Press, 1978.

135. "Brown After 25 Years." *Emory Law Journal* 28 (1979): 933-47.

136. "The College Presidency: Life Between a Rock and a Hard Place." *Change* 11 (May-June 1979): 43-47.

137. [Commentary.] In *25 Years Since Brown: A Commemorative Booklet,* edited by Anne Dowling, 55. New York: NAACP Legal Defense and Educational Fund, 1979.

138. "A Harbinger of Hope." *Michigan Quarterly Review* 18 (1979): 183-85.

139. "Human Development and the Future in the Third and Fourth Worlds." In *Human Development Through Social Change: Proceedings of St. Francis Xavier University's International Symposium Commemorating the Fiftieth Anniversary of the Antigonish Movement, 1928-1978, Antigonish, Nova Scotia, Canada,* edited by Philip Milner, 177-82. Antigonish, N.S.: Formac Publishing Co., 1979.

140. "In Memoriam." In *A Celebration of the Memory and the Love of John Hilton Knowles, 1926-1979,* Harvard University, The Memorial Church, Friday, 16 March 1979, 7-9. Cambridge, Mass.: Harvard University, 1979. UNDA: PPHS.

Hesburgh's eulogy for John Hilton Knowles, physician
and administrator of Massachusetts General Hospital,
and president of the Rockefeller Foundation. "He died
in full flight, like a wild bird on the wing, sensing
the far horizon, savoring the beauty at hand, but still
reaching out eagerly for the vaster beauty beyond."
--p. 9.

141.   "Meaning of Religion After 50." *50 Plus* 19 (December
1979): 33.

142.   Hesburgh, Theodore M., and James P. Grant. "Overview
Essay: The United States and World Development,
1979." In *The United States and World Development:
Agenda, 1979*, by Martin M. McLaughlin and the Staff
of the Overseas Development Council, 1-14. New York:
Praeger, 1979.

143.   "A Priest in the Land of the Dragon." *Notre Dame
Magazine* 8 (October 1979): 20-25.

Hesburgh provides insight into China's economic
development, energy production, agricultural
organization, educational system, and population
control in his diary account of 16 days spent in the
People's Republic of China. With Jim and Ethel Grant,
Jean Wilkowski, and Lynn and Dianne Pascoe of the State
Department, they were preparing for the U.N. Conference
on Science and Technology to be held in Vienna in
August, 1979.

144.   Hesburgh, Theodore M. and Peter J. Henriot. "Science
and Technology for a Global Society." *Current* 218
(December 1979): 52-58.

145.   Hesburgh, Theodore M., and Peter J. Henriot. "Science
and Technology for Development: The Role of the
United States." *Social Education* 43 (October 1979):
433-36.

146. "Statement by Theodore M. Hesburgh, C.S.C., President, Notre Dame University and Chairman, United States Commission on Civil Rights." In *Equal Employment: Mandate and Challenge*, by Francis Albert Korngay, 171-73. New York: Vantage Press, 1979.

147. "Technology Has to Be Profitable for Those Who Develop It, But Reasonably Profitable." *Ceres* 12 (May-June 1979): 39-41.

148. "A Vision of Excellence At Last Within Reach." *Notre Dame Magazine* 8 (February 1979): 68-70.

Hesburgh summarizes the progress of the Campaign for Notre Dame, a $130 million development drive entering phase three. He considers endowment the key to stability and survival amid constantly rising costs.

1980-1988

149. "Address given . . . at the 174th Commencement of Rensselaer Polytechnic Institute, May 16, 1980." Speech reprint. Troy, N.Y.: Rensselaer Polytechnic Institute, Office of University Relations, 1980. UNDA.

Demonstrates the value of the spirit of voluntarism in the context of aid to Cambodian refugees.

150. "The Catholic University in Today's World." *Origins* 9 (April 3, 1980): 681-84.

First annual Elizabeth Ann Seton Lecture, Seton Hall University, South Orange, N.J., 12 March 1980. Also published under title "The Catholic University in the Modern Context" in *Catholic Mind*, vol. 78, October 1980, pp. 18-25.

151. "Charter Day Address." In *Charter Day 1980: Exercises Commemorating the Two Hundred and Eighty-Seventh Anniversary of the Granting of the Royal Charter for the Establishment of the College of William and Mary in Virginia, and the 200th Anniversary of the Reorganization of the College, Saturday, February Ninth, 1980*, 1-8. Williamsburg, Va.: The College of William and Mary, 1980. UNDA.

Address on "The Future of Liberal Education." Liberally educated students should learn to think clearly, logically, and deeply about the meaning and purpose of human life.

152. "Eulogy for Rev. John J. Cavanaugh, C.S.C." *Notre Dame Report* 9 (1980): 230-32.

Eulogy delivered 31 December 1979, for Rev. John J. Cavanaugh, C.S.C., fourteenth president of Notre Dame. Hesburgh extols his many virtues, particularly his integrity. Also issued separately as a booklet by the Office of the President, University of Notre Dame.

153. "Morality and Foreign Policy." *Worldview* 23 (1980): 30.

154. "Presidential Leadership: The Keystone for Advancement." In *Presidential Leadership in Advancement Activities*, edited by James L. Fisher, 1-8. New Directions for Institutional Advancement, vol. 8. San Francisco: Jossey-Bass, 1980.

155. "Reflections on Voluntarism in America: Regulations Must Promote the Common Goal." *Vital Speeches* 46 (1 June 1980): 484-87.

Delivered 21 April 1980 at the Volunteer Leaders Conference of United Way of America, Toronto, Canada.

156. "Service to Others." In *Representative American Speeches: 1979-1980,* edited by Waldo W. Braden, 180-86. The Reference Shelf, vol. 52, no. 5. New York: H. W. Wilson, 1980.

Hesburgh discusses service to others in terms of the volunteer spirit. The greatest freedom we enjoy today is the freedom to choose our own goals for our lives, serving others in a spirit of compassion, commitment, and consecration. Address delivered at the 110th Commencement, University of Utah, Salt Lake City, 9 June 1979.

157. "Theodore M. Hesburgh." In *Messages to the Next Civilization,* edited by Norman E. Hunt, with an introduction by Norman Cousins. Arlington, Va.: Privately printed for the World Federalists Association, 1980.

Given the tremendous power now available for violence and destruction, Hesburgh sees change as imperative to prevent the ultimate end of civilization.

158. "President's Address to the Faculty." *Notre Dame Report* 10 (2 January 1981): 278-85.

Remarks and address at the meeting of the general faculty in Washington Hall, 13 October 1980. Text: "The Future of Liberal Education." Hesburgh discusses the qualities of a liberal education. He concludes that "the future of liberal education is somehow dictated by the most profound need of our age: to rediscover man and the meaning of human life, to give meaning, purpose, and direction to our days, to reinvigorate our society and our world by the kind of human leadership that can only come from a human person conscious of his ultimate destiny, his vision beyond time, his idealism that transcends power, money, or pleasure; ultimately, the awareness of what men and women can be and the determination to recreate the

world in that vision."--pp. 284-85. Reprinted in
slightly different form as "The Future of Liberal
Education," *Change*, vol. 13, April 1981, pp. 36-40;
and "Liberal Education: What Is Its Future?" *Current*,
vol. 234, July-August, 1981, pp. 3-11. Translated as
"O Futuro da Educação Liberal," *Humanidades*, vol. 1,
October-December 1982, pp. 42-48.

159. "President's Address to the Faculty." *Notre Dame
Report* 11 (13 November 1981): 139-43.

Address delivered 12 October 1981 in Washington
Hall. Text: "A Great Catholic University: A
Persistent Dream." Hesburgh describes his vision
of a great Catholic university as one demanding faith,
a concern for values, intellectual growth, moral
integrity, and a quest for excellence. Text also
distributed as a booklet by the Department of Public
Relations and Information, University of Notre Dame,
in 1982.

160. "President"s Statement on the International Year of
Disabled Persons." *Notre Dame Report* 10 (20 February
1981): 337-38.

Hesburgh cites past legislation which assures education
for handicapped children, and draws attention to the
need to attend to the plight of the mentally retarded
and the physically handicapped.

161. "Should Congress Adopt 'Employer Sanctions' to
Control the Number of Illegal Aliens in the U.S.?"
Congressional Digest 60 (October 1981): 246ff.

162. "A Call to the Conscience of the University
Community." *Center Magazine* 15 (1982): 44.

163. "The Capability for Unique Contributions." In
*Multinational Managers and Poverty in the Third
World*, edited by Lee A. Tavis, 94-101. Notre Dame,

Ind.: University of Notre Dame Press, 1982.

164. "The Catholic University Today." In *In Words
      Commemorated: Essays Celebrating the Centennial of
      Incarnate Word College, San Antonio, Texas*, edited by
      Alacoque Power, 13-24. San Antonio: Incarnate Word
      College, 1982.

      Hesburgh reviews the historical development of
      Catholic universities, beginning with the University
      of Paris in 1205. He describes at some length the
      essence of a Catholic university.

165. "The Elections in El Salvador." *America* 146 (1 May
      1982): 336-37.

166. "On Voluntarism." *Scouting* 70 (March-April 1982):
      19.

167. "President's Address to the Faculty." *Notre Dame
      Report* 12 (15 October 1982): 76-82.

      "Preparing for the Millennium." Address given at the
      general faculty meeting on 4 October 1982. Reviews
      final report of the findings of the Carnegie Council on
      Policy Studies in Higher Education. During the next
      two decades administrators must make hard choices on
      quality, balance, integrity, dynamism, and other
      factors essential for survivial. Text also issued
      separately as a booklet by the Department of Public
      Relations and Information, University of Notre Dame,
      1982. Reprinted in *Origins*, vol. 12, November 4,
      1982, pp. 337-42; *Current Issues in Higher Education*,
      vol, 3, Winter 1983, pp. 10-14; and *Change*, vol. 15,
      October 1983, pp. 14-17.

168. "Rev. Theodore Hesburgh, President, University of
      Notre Dame." *World Tennis* 29 (January 1982): 41.

On sportsmanship.

169. Review of *The Fate of the Earth*, by Jonathan Schell.
      New Catholic World 225 (July-August 1982): 193.

170. "The Role of Voluntarism in America: An Address . . .
      Before the Business-Higher Education Forum."
      Washington, D.C.: Business-Higher Education Forum,
      1982.

      Address delivered 15 January 1982. Voluntarism and
      government aid should be synergistic, working together
      rather than at cross purposes. The Cambodian crisis
      exemplified an effective cooperative effort.

      ERIC ED 222 097.

171. "The Triumph of a Tortured People." *Notre Dame
      Magazine* 11 (May 1982): 19-23.

      Hesburgh, one of seven members of the U.S. State
      Department's official delegation sent to observe the
      national elections held in El Salvador, records his
      observations on the explosive situation in journal
      entries dated 25 March to 30 March 1982.

172. "We Study War, Why Not Study Peace?" *Common Cause* 8
      (April 1982): 6.

173. "Eulogy for Joseph O'Meara." *Notre Dame Report* 12
      (1983): 501-502.

      Hesburgh delivers his eulogy for Joseph O'Meara, Dean
      of the Law School, in Sacred Heart Church on 21 June
      1983.

174. "Finding an Identity and a Future." *Change* 15
      (October 1983): 15-17.

Hesburgh observes that "the general lack of concern on the part of higher education for elementary and secondary education is at the heart of the nationwide educational crisis."--p. 16.

175. "The Laetare Medal: 1883-1983." In *Laetare Medal Centennial: 1883-1983, University of Notre Dame*, edited by Michael Garvey, 1-2. Notre Dame, Ind.: Department of Information Services, University of Notre Dame, 1983.

176. "The Longing for Peace Is Deep." *Notre Dame Magazine* 12 (May 1983): 27.

Text of a statement signed by Hesburgh and ten international religious leaders on 15 January 1983 in Vienna. "Lasting peace can only be based upon global justice, respect for the dignity of each person, a conversion of mind and heart regarding war and peace and, finally, the Creator's call for reconciliation between estranged peoples."

177. "Nov. 22, 1963: A Day Beyond Forgetting." *People* 20 (28 November 1983): 12ff.

Hesburgh pays tribute to John F. Kennedy.

178. "President's Address to Faculty." *Notre Dame Report* 13 (1983): 77-83.

Address subsequently given as the keynote address entitled "The Moral Dimensions of Higher Education," Joint Meeting of the American Council on Education and the Association of Colleges and Universities of Canada, Toronto, 13 October 1983.

179. "Recommended Reading." *Notre Dame Magazine* 12 (February 1983): 63.

Among other titles, Hesburgh recommends *The Fate of the Earth* by Jonathan Schell as "the best description thus far of the threat to humanity posed by nuclear weapons."

180. "Reflections on Priesthood." In *Holy Cross: Perspectives and Possibilities*, 1-4. Notre Dame, Ind.: Vocation Director, University of Notre Dame, 1983?

Commencement address, Immaculate Conception Seminary, Darlington, New Jersey, 11 September 1983. Hesburgh considers the priest as a mediator who bridges the gap between the human and divine, between time and eternity. Reprinted in the *Serran*, March 1985, p. 4ff.

181. "Save Our Schools." *U.S. Catholic* 48 (March 1983): 45-46.

Hesburgh responds to a November article by Kris Tuberty, "Catholic Grade Schools: An Idea Whose Time Has Passed?" Hesburgh objects to the statement that Catholic schools in 1982 are anachronisms. He sees the unique role of the Catholic school as evangelization, in keeping with the Church's social justice mission.

182. "To Compete with Honor." *Notre Dame Magazine* 12 (February 1983): 21.

Hesburgh observes that in intercollegiate sports, improprieties are commonplace and widespread. Quality education for athletes should remain the highest priority. "Players will learn early that victory is the fruit of effort, discipline, and teamwork, of overcoming discouragement and gaining self-confidence."--p. 21.

183. "The Catholic University in the Modern Context." In *Pro Fide et Iustitia: Festschrift für Agostino Kardinal Casaroli zum 70. Geburtstag*, edited by Herbert Schambeck, 621-28. Berlin: Duncker & Humbolt,

1984.

184. "Dean Joseph O'Meara." *Notre Dame Law Review* 59,
no. 3 (1984): [vi-x].

Hesburgh pays final tribute to Joseph O'Meara, Dean
of the Notre Dame Law School from 1952-1968, who
harbored "a fierce partisanship for justice."

185. "A Genesis Answer." *Notre Dame Magazine* 13 (Late
Winter 1984): 2.

Hesburgh responds to "The Genesis Question" by Jon
Franklin (*Notre Dame Magazine*, December, 1983),
and reaffirms his belief in the possibility of extraterrestrial intelligence.

186. "Higher Education and the Nuclear Crisis." *Bulletin
of the Atomic Scientists* 40 (December 1984): 3s.

187. "Nuclear War: Its Consequences and Prevention."
Origins 14 (6 December 1984): 415.

On 26 November 1984 Hesburgh issued a statement on
behalf of thirty scientists and religious leaders who met
at the invitation of the International Council of
Scientific Unions and the University of Notre
Dame's Interfaith Academy of Peace. "In the
search for effective means of escape from the threat
of nuclear disaster, it is important to begin with
the necessity for fundamental changes in international relations, especially in the relations
between the Soviet Union and the United States."
--p. 415.

188. "Reflections on Cuomo: The Secret Consensus." *Notre
Dame Journal of Law, Ethics, and Public Policy* 1
(1984): 53-56.

Response to Governor Mario Cuomo's address on religion and politics at Notre Dame. The widespread uneasiness about 1,500,000 abortions a year on demand "is not an exclusively Catholic malaise."

189. Review of *The Challenge of Peace: God's Promise and Our Response*, by the National Conference of Catholic Bishops. *Journal of Law and Religion* 2 (1984): 435-41.

Hesburgh summarizes his own efforts to bring together scientific and religious leaders. He comments at some length on the U.S. bishops' pastoral letter, which he considers "the finest document that the American hierarchy has ever produced."

190. "Social Responsibility of Graduate Education." *Notre Dame Report* 14 (November 30, 1984): 229-34.

President's address to the faculty delivered 8 October 1984. Hesburgh emphasizes the importance of academic excellence, and the need for commitment to service. Published also as part of the proceedings of the twenty-fourth annual meeting of the Council of Graduate Schools in the United States, 5-8 December 1984, in *Graduate Education--A Quantity of Quality for the Needs of the Nation*, 81-89. Washington, D.C.: Council of Graduate Schools in the United States, 1985?

191. "Statement on Special Libraries and Information Centers in 2009: An Informed Speculation." In *Information and Special Libraries in 2009: Informed Speculations*, edited by Judy Genesen and David E. King, 13. Chicago: Special Libraries Association, Illinois Chapter, 1984.

Hesburgh predicts that the library of the future will resemble an electronic office. Librarians will expedite information transfer by linking users to appropriate information sources.

192. "Vision and Faith Bind Religious Communities and Education." *Momentum* 15 (September 1984): 20-21.

   Recalls Rev. Edward F. Sorin's spiritual assets of vision and faith, and the unique contributions which religious communities have made to Catholic education in the United States.

193. "A Well-Kept Secret." *Notre Dame Magazine* 13 (Autumn 1984): 30.

   Hesburgh comments on Governor Mario Cuomo's speech on religion and politics at Notre Dame in September 1984. A "moral consensus does exist for a stricter abortion law . . . . On the abortion issue today, a minority is imposing its belief on a demonstrable majority."--p. 30.

194. "Another Part of the Kingdom." *Notre Dame Magazine* 14 (Spring 1985): 65-67.

   Hesburgh describes his trip to the Far East, including Beijing and Tianjin. In China, he discovers the country's new attitudes toward education and religion.

195. "Catholic Higher Education: A Personal Reflection." In *Where We Are: American Catholics in the 1980s: A Celebration for Philip Scharper*, edited by Michael Glazier, 192-99. Wilmington: Michael Glazier, 1985.

   Reviews the growth and development of Notre Dame in terms of student graduates, budget, physical facilities, a lay Board of Trustees, co-education, and a heightened sense of service.

196. "Commencement Address: Rensselaer Polytechnic Institute, May 16, 1980." In *"I Am Honored To Be Here Today . . . ." Commencement Speeches by Notable Personalities*, edited by Donald Grunewald, 115-21. New York: Oceana, 1985.

Hesburgh emphasizes the value of voluntarism, citing
Albert Schweitzer as a great volunteer.

197.   "Father Theodore M. Hesburgh: The View from Notre
Dame." In *Re-Imagining American Catholicism: The
American Bishops and Their Pastoral Letter*, by Eugene
Kennedy, 143-59. New York: Vintage Books, 1985.

198.   "Liberal Education: A Human Imperative." *College
Digest* 2 (December 1985): Inside front cover, 41.

199.   "President's Address to Faculty." *Notre Dame Report*
15 (15 November 1985): 129-32.

Hesburgh's thirty-fourth address to the faculty on
2 October 1985. Hesburgh stresses academic
excellence, and reiterates Rev. Edward F. Sorin's
dream: "'. . . if there is ever to be a great Catholic
university in America, it will be *here*.' Vision
alone gives us only a visionary, in the pejorative
sense of that word. But join vision and faith, and
mountains begin to move." Text also issued separately
as a booklet under the title *Vision & Faith: The Inner
Life of Notre Dame*, by the Department of Public
Relations and Information, University of Notre Dame.

200.   "The Priest as Mediator and Ambassador." In *Between
God and Caesar: Priests, Sisters and Political Office
in the United States*, edited by Madonna Kolbenschlag,
282-90. New York: Paulist Press, 1985.

201.   "Religious, Scientific Leaders On Arms Race."
Bulletin of the Atomic Scientists 41 (April 1985):
49-50.

Hesburgh documents efforts to gather scientific and
religious leaders together to make common cause
against the nuclear threat to humanity. Includes
conference statement composed by a group of
scientists and religious leaders.

202. "Rev. Theodore M. Hesburgh." In *A Celebration of Teachers*," 17. Urbana: National Council of Teachers of English, 1985.

Hesburgh recalls his student days and renders words of praise for Sister Veronica, his English teacher at Most Holy Rosary High School, Syracuse, New York. She "pointed me in a direction that has brought me untold pleasure in reading great books and even some very hard hours of trying to write readable prose." Also published in the new edition, 1986, p. 24.

203. "Reverend Theodore M. Hesburgh, CSC." In *Christian Jewish Relations: A Documentary Survey* 18 (September 1985): 23-27.

Hesburgh contributes to "*Nostra Aetate* Twenty Years On: A Symposium," published by the Institute of Jewish Affairs in association with the World Jewish Congress.

204. Review of *The Bishops and Nuclear Weapons: The Catholic Pastoral Letter on War and Peace,* by James E. Dougherty. *Political Science Quarterly* 100 (Summer 1985): 317.

Hesburgh considers Dougherty's work "a judicious study of the theological launching sites of the pastoral letter: pacifism and just war theory and development.--p. 317.

205. "The Role of Business in Higher Education." *Pro Education* 2 (April 1985): 12-19.

206. "The Role of the Academy in a Nuclear Age." In *Contemporary Issues In Higher Education*, edited by John B. Bennett and J. W. Peltason, 247-66. New York: American Council on Education, 1985.

Discusses the function of academic institutions in shaping the future, particularly with regard to the moral dimensions of higher education and the nuclear threat.

207.   "Theodore Hesburgh." In *God &*, by Terrance A. Sweeney, 169-172. Minneapolis: Winston Press, 1985.

Hesburgh reveals his innermost thoughts about God.

208.   "Theodore Hesburgh Joins Board of Advisors." *Planetary Report* 5 (July/August 1985): 3.

In accepting membership on the Board of Advisors of the Planetary Society, Hesburgh speculates on the nature of God's created universe and affirms his belief in the possibility of extraterrestrial intelligence.

209.   "Are Religious Orders Obsolete? Theodore Hesburgh Responds." *Critic* 41 (Winter 1986): 9-11.

"I would argue that the question is not so much whether religious life is obsolete as much as whether permanent lifetime commitments are possible in our age. I happen to firmly believe not only that they are possible, but that they are essential."--p. 9.

210.   "Catholic Education in America." *America* 155 (4 October 1986): 160-64.

Hesburgh praises the Golden Age of American Catholic education and the magnificent contribution of American religious women. He accentuates the most important factor for the future of the whole enterprise: "guard your Catholic character as you would your life."--p. 164. Address delivered at the National Catholic Educational Association, Washington, D.C., 4 June 1986.

211. "Dear Pax Christi U.S.A." *Pax Christi USA* 11
     (Winter 1986): 23.

     Excerpt from Hesburgh's response to a mailgram from
     Pax Christi protesting the construction of the
     Clarke War Memorial at the University of Notre Dame.

212. "The Dream and Reality of Justice in America."
     Capitol University Law Review 15 (Spring 1986): 411-
     16.

213. "The End of Apartheid in America." *The George
     Washington Law Review* 54 (January & March 1986): 244-
     52.

214. "President's Address to Faculty." *Notre Dame Report*
     16 (14 November 1986): 98-102.

     Hesburgh's final presidential address to the Notre
     Dame faculty on 13 October 1986, the Feast of St.
     Edward. Describes in detail the life, work, and
     vision of Notre Dame's founder, Rev. Edward F.
     Sorin, C.S.C.

215. "Quality and Equality of Education." *Educational
     Forum* 50 (Spring 1986): 313-16.

     Hesburgh asserts that "equality speaks to the
     opportunity to have the best," citing the career of
     Leontyne Price, Metropolitan Opera star, who as a
     young black girl in Mississippi had talent, but no
     opportunity until a white family provided her with the
     means to the highest quality education in music.

216. "Troubled Son." *Esquire* 105 (April 1986): 15.

     Hesburgh praises powerful article by Rian Malan
     entitled "My Traitor's Heart" (*Esquire,* November,
     1985, pp. 75-91) which portrays the life of an
     Afrikaner caught in moral conflict.

217. "The Vatican and American Catholic Higher Education."
      America 155 (1 November 1986): 247-50; 263.

      A detailed analysis and critique of the proposed
      Schema of the Congregation on Catholic Education
      addressed to Catholic colleges and universities
      throughout the world.

218. "A Family in Crisis." *Woman's Day* (August 4, 1987):
      82-83.

      Hesburgh responds to a letter from a woman deeply
      concerned about her seventeen-year-old daughter who
      is four months pregnant.

219. "If I Had Five Minutes With the Pope." *America* 157
      (12-19 September 1987): 129-30.

      Hesburgh urges the Holy Father to listen to bishops,
      priests, women religious educators, married couples,
      theologians, lay women, and others with an open mind.

220. "The Opinion Corner: Peace Corps-ROTC Style." *Journal
      of Student Financial Aid* 17 (Spring 1987): 59-60.

221. "Academic Leadership." In *Leaders on Leadership:
      The College Presidency*, edited by James L. Fisher
      and Martha W. Tack, 5-8. New Directions for Higher
      Education, vol. 61. San Francisco: Jossey-Bass,
      1988.

      Leaders need "a clear and challenging vision, a magic
      with words, the ability to motivate others, courage to
      stay on course, and the persistence not to lose hope."

222. "Presidential Science Advising: A Memoir and a
      Prescription." In *Science and Technology Advice
      to the President, Congress, and Judiciary*, edited
      by William T. Golden, 165-66. New York: Pergamon
      Press, 1988.

Hesburgh laments the disintegration of sound scientific advice to presidential leaders, evident in launching the Strategic Defense Initiative and other programs. He prescribes reinstatement of a highly qualified science advisor and a President's Science Advisory Committee during the next administration.

223. "Really Being Christian." *Notre Dame Magazine* 17 (Autumn 1988): 2.

In a letter, Hesburgh describes his visit with José Napoleón Duarte in his hospital room at Walter Reed the night before his operation for cancer. Duarte prayed for "the guerillas" and asked Hesburgh to express his thanks to all Notre Dame alumni for their prayers and messages.

Forewords, Prefaces, and Introductions by Theodore M. Hesburgh

1950-1959

224. Introduction to *The Mystery of Woman: Essays on the Mother of God*, edited by Edward D. O'Connor. Notre Dame, Ind.: University of Notre Dame Press, 1956.

225. Foreword to "Problems and Responsibilities of Desegregation: A Symposium." *Notre Dame Lawyer* 34, no. 5 (Symposium, 1959): Preliminary page.

    Addressing members of a symposium on desegregation, Hesburgh expresses his hope that future leaders will "become more dedicated to what man is--made in the image and likeness of God, something a little less than the angels . . . ."--Preliminary page.

1960-1969

226. Foreword to *Love Is Life: A Catholic Marriage Handbook*, by François Dantec. Revised and adapted by Albert L. Schlitzer. Notre Dame, Ind.: University of Notre Dame Press, 1963.

227. Introduction to *The Variety of Catholic Attitudes*, by Theodore L. Westow. New York: Herder and Herder,

1963.

228. Preface and introduction to *The Person in Contemporary Society: A Symposium on the Occasion of the Dedication of the Memorial Library, University of Notre Dame, May 7, 1964.* Notre Dame, Ind.: University of Notre Dame Press, 1964.

229. Preface to *The Idea of the Catholic University.* International Federation of Catholic Universities. Land O'Lakes, Wis.: n.p., 1967.

As president of the International Federation of Catholic Universities, Hesburgh introduces this study document which addresses the nature and role of the contemporary Catholic university.

230. Foreword to *Catholic Education Faces Its Future*, by Neil Gerard McCluskey. Garden City: Doubleday, 1968.

"As Catholic education faces its future, those of us involved therein will need to have the qualities of the pioneer: vision, courage, confidence, and a great hope inspired by faith and freshened by love. The present book challenges its readers to take up the work of tomorrow with this kind of intelligent optimism."

231. Introduction to *The Citizen Christian*, by James F. Andrews. New York: Sheed and Ward, 1968.

232. Foreword to *Prejudice U.S.A.*, edited by Charles Y. Glock and Ellen Siegelman. New York: Praeger, 1969.

Hesburgh presents a lucid essay on the nature of prejudice. His emphasis is theological, "tempered by eleven years of viewing the practical results of prejudice as a charter member of the U.S. Commission on Civil Rights."--p. v.

1970-1979

233. Foreword to *Evolving Religious Careers*, edited by
Willis E. Bartlett. Washington, D.C.: Center for
Applied Research in the Apostolate, 1970.

234. Preface to *The Catholic University: A Modern
Appraisal*, edited by Neil G. McCluskey. Notre Dame,
Ind.: University of Notre Dame Press, 1970.

In a lengthy preface, Hesburgh discusses theology as
queen of the sciences in the Middle Ages and the role
of the Catholic university in the modern world.

235. Foreword to *People Who Care: An Illustrated History
of Human Compassion*, by Heinz Vonhoff. Philadelphia:
Fortress Press, 1971.

236. Foreword to *Toward a Free Housing Market*, by Daniel
Jay Baum, in collaboration with Karen Orloff Kaplan.
Coral Gables, Fla.: University of Miami Press, 1971.

237. Foreword to *The Adolescent Gap: Research Findings on
Drug Using and Non-Drug Using Teens*, by Edward M.
Scott. Springfield, Ill.: Charles C. Thomas, 1972.

Hesburgh finds this work refreshing in its approach to
the drug problem. Scott uses the personal experiences
of young people to provide information, insight, and
understanding to a problem of growing national concern.

238. Preface to *The Future of Notre Dame: Three Preliminary
Questions*, by M. A. Fitzsimons. Notre Dame, Ind.:
Department of Information Services, University of
Notre Dame, 1972.

239. Introduction to *The United States and the Developing
World: Agenda for Action, 1973*. Robert E. Hunter,
Project Director. Washington, D.C.: Overseas Develop-
ment Council, 1973.

240. Foreword to *Onward To Victory: A Chronicle of the Alumni of the University of Notre Dame du Lac, 1842-1973*, by James E. Armstrong. Notre Dame, Ind.: The University of Notre Dame, 1974.

241. Foreword to *The U.S. and the Developing World: Agenda for Action, 1974*, by James W. Howe. New York: Praeger, 1974.

242. "Preface: Fiftieth Anniversary Volume." *Notre Dame Lawyer* 50, no. 1 (October 1974): 6-16.

     Discusses *Brown v. Board of Education*, the Civil Rights Act of 1964, the busing of schoolchildren, and desegregation.

243. Foreword to *Notes From a College President: Issues in American Higher Education*, by Louis C. Vaccaro. Boston: Beacon Hill Press, 1975.

244. Foreword to *The U.S. and World Development: Agenda for Action, 1975*, by James W. Howe. New York: Praeger, 1975.

245. "Introduction: American Churches and Global Justice." In *Global Justice & Development: Report of the Aspen Interreligious Consultation, Aspen, Colorado, June 1974*, sponsored by the Overseas Development Council with the support of the Aspen Institute for Humanistic Studies and the Johnson Foundation, 1-8. Washington, D.C.: Overseas Development Council, 1975.

246. Introduction to *The U.S. and World Development: Agenda for Action, 1976*, by Roger D. Hansen and the Staff of the Overseas Development Council. New York: Praeger, 1976.

247. "Welcome." In *Evangelization in the American Context*, edited by David B. Burrell and Franzita Kane, 8-13. Notre Dame, Ind.: University of Notre Dame, 1976.

Symposium on evangelization held 11-13 January 1976.

248. Foreword to *The Immigrant Experience: Faith, Hope, and the Golden Door,* by Edward Wakin. Huntington, Ind.: Our Sunday Visitor, 1977.

Hesburgh delineates several instances of injustice in immigration laws. He supports President Carter's initiative in shaping new, more humane immigration policies.

249. Foreword to *Reconciliation After Vietnam: A Program of Relief for Vietnam Era Draft and Military Offenders,* by Lawrence M. Baskir and William A. Strauss. Notre Dame, Ind.: University of Notre Dame, 1977. (Also issued under imprint: University of Notre Dame Press.)

250. Foreword to *The Search for Extraterrestrial Intelligence* (SETI), edited by Philip Morrison, John Billingham, and John Wolfe. NASA Special Publication: NASA SP-419. Washington, D.C.: National Aeronautics and Space Administration, Scientific and Technical Information Office, 1977.

SuDoc no. NAS 1.21.419.

251. Introduction to *The United States and World Development Agenda, 1977,* by John W. Sewell and the Staff of the Overseas Development Council. New York: Praeger, 1977.

252. Foreword to *Chance and Circumstance: The Draft, the War and the Vietnam Generation,* by Lawrence M. Baskir and William A. Strauss. New York: Alfred A. Knopf, 1978.

253. Foreword to *Four Hasidic Masters and Their Struggle Against Melancholy,* by Elie Wiesel. Ward-Phillips Lectures in English Language and Literature, no. 9.

Notre Dame, Ind.: University of Notre Dame Press, 1978.

Hesburgh comments at some length on Wiesel's style, his work, and the Jewish and Christian traditions. "In these lectures it makes little difference that the Jew waits for the Messiah while the Christian waits for the Messiah's Second Coming. Both wait. It is the human condition. It demands a difficult and balanced response. Jew and Christian can learn much from each other about the proper way to wait."--p. xv.

254. Preface to *Lord Hear Our Prayer*, compiled by Thomas McNally and William G. Storey. Notre Dame, Ind.: Ave Maria Press, 1978.

255. Foreword to *Chaucerian Problems and Perspective: Essays Presented to Paul E. Beichner, C.S.C.*, edited by Edward Vasta and Zacharias P. Thundy. Notre Dame, Ind.: University of Notre Dame Press, 1979.

256. Foreword to *Church and Campus: Legal Issues in Religiously Affiliated Higher Education*, by Philip R. Moots and Edward McGlynn Gaffney, Jr. Notre Dame, Ind.: University of Notre Dame Press, 1979.

257. Foreword to *Mission to Latin America: The Successes and Failures of a Twentieth Century Crusade*, by Gerald M. Costello. Maryknoll, N.Y.: Orbis Books, 1979.

258. Preface to *Science and Technology for Development*. United States. Delegation to the U.N. Conference on Science and Technology for Development, Vienna, 1979. U.S. Dept. of State. International Organization and Conference series, 139. U.S. Dept. of State Publication 8966. Washington, D.C.: Dept. of State, 1979.

SuDoc no. S1.70:139.

1980-1988

259. Foreword to *Abortion Parley*. National Conference on Abortion (1979: University of Notre Dame), edited by James Tunstead Burtchaell. Kansas City: Andrews and McMeel, 1980.

260. Foreword to *Reach Out and Touch: Hope for Adults and Youth*, by T. R. Haney. Waldrick, N.J.: Arena Lettres, 1980.

261. Foreword to *This Church, These Times: The Roman Catholic Church Since Vatican II*, by Franklin McMahon and Francis X. Murphy. Chicago: Association Press, 1980.

   "The postconciliar church is not more secure, more safe, more peaceful, or more orderly. But it is a better church--more Christlike and less worldly . . . more interested in compassion than condemnation, praying for forgiveness for ourselves while pardoning others."

262. Introduction to *The United States and World Development: Agenda 1980*, by John W. Sewell and the Staff of the Overseas Development Council. Praeger Special Studies. New York: Praeger, 1980.

263. Preface to *A Song of Pilgrimage: The Life and Spirit of Mother Marianne of Molokai*, by Sister Mary Laurence Hanley and O. A. Bushnell. Chicago: Franciscan Herald Press, 1980.

264. Foreword to *Symposium: Immigration and Refugee Law. Notre Dame Lawyer* 56, no. 4 (April 1981): 614-17.

   Hesburgh discusses four broad areas which constitute the work of the Select Commission on Immigration: the undocumented/illegal alien; alien protections--procedural reform; refugees and mass first asylum; and the nonimmigrant.

100   Theodore M. Hesburgh

265. Preface to *Japan and the United States in a Turbulent World: Myths & Reality*, edited by Yusaku Furuhashi. ITT Key Issues Lecture Series. West Babylon, N.Y.: KCG Productions, 1981.

266. Preface to *New Immigrants: Portraits in Passage*, by Thomas Bentz. New York: Pilgrim Press, 1981.

267. Foreword to *Multinational Managers and Poverty in the Third World*, edited by Lee A. Tavis. Notre Dame, Ind.: University of Notre Dame Press, 1982.

268. Foreword to *The Splendid Risk: An Existential Approach to Christian Fulfillment* by Bernard I. Mullahy. Notre Dame, Ind.: University of Notre Dame, 1982.

Hesburgh views Mullahy's analysis of the contemporary spiritual climate as deeply influenced by existentialism and personalism. Mullahy cultivates a holistic spirituality based upon a Teilhardian vision of all creation moving toward the Omega point.

269. Introduction to *Monique's Menus: A Cookbook of Oriental and Continental Cuisine*, by Monique Kobayashi. N.p.: For the Benefit of the American Cancer Society, Indiana Division, 1982.

270. Foreword to *Catholics and Nuclear War: A Commentary on The Challenge of Peace: The U.S. Catholic Bishops' Pastoral Letter on War and Peace*, edited by Philip J. Murnion. New York: Crossroads, 1983.

271. Foreword to *Letters to Bill on University Administration*, by George Lynn Cross. Norman: University of Oklahoma Press, 1983.

Hesburgh summarizes highlights of the life and work of George Lynn Cross who became the seventh president of the University of Oklahoma in 1944. Hesburgh

describes Cross's concern with the administration of
intercollegiate athletics, and his effort to establish
more reasonable regulations for athletic aid.

272. Foreword to *The Governance of Jesuit Colleges in the
      United States, 1920-1970,* by Paul A. FitzGerald.
      Notre Dame, Ind.: University of Notre Dame Press,
      1984.

273. Foreword to *Social Issues in Business: Strategic and
      Public Policy Perspectives* by Fred Luthans, Richard
      M. Hodgetts, and Kenneth R. Thompson. 4th ed. New
      York: Macmillan, 1984.

274. Foreword to *Christians and Jews: The Eternal Bond,* by
      Stuart E. Rosenberg. New York: Ungar, 1985.

275. Foreword to *Reflections in the Dome,* edited by James
      O'Rourke IV. Notre Dame, Ind.: Juniper Press, 1985.

276. Introduction to *Faculty Handbook, University of Notre
      Dame.* 13th ed. Notre Dame, Ind.: Office of the
      Provost, University of Notre Dame, 1985.

      In his classic introduction, issued for the last time
      in this edition, Hesburgh elaborates on the Catholic
      character of the university, portraying it in terms
      of a beacon, bridge, and crossroads "where all the
      vital intellectual currents of our times meet in
      dialogue, where the Church confronts the modern world
      with all its insights and all its anguishes, with all
      its possibilities and all its despairs, where the
      great issues of the Church in the world today are
      plumbed to their depths."--p. 3. This introduction
      appears in previous editions of the *Faculty Handbook,*
      and in its predecessor, the *University of Notre Dame
      Faculty Manual,* 1967.

277. Introduction to *The Jesus Connection: To Triumph Over
      Anti-Semitism,* by Leonard C. Yaseen. New York:

Crossroad, 1985.

278.   "Presentation." In *The Church and Culture Since Vatican II: The Experience of North and Latin America*, edited by Joseph Gremillion. Notre Dame, Ind.: University of Notre Dame Press, 1985.

279.   Foreword to *The Papacy and the Middle East: The Role of the Holy See in the Arab-Israeli Conflict, 1962-1984*, by George Emile Irani. Notre Dame, Ind.: University of Notre Dame Press, 1986.

Commenting on the value of this work in its objective analysis, Hesburgh states that "Irani has accomplished a kind of tour de force in bringing together the Jewish, Christian, and Islamic perspectives."--p. ix.

280.   Preface to *Duarte: My Story*, by José Napoleón Duarte, with Diana Page. New York: Putnam, 1986.

In a spirit of sympathy and understanding, Hesburgh reflects on Duarte's difficult position in a "culture of violence." Hesburgh asks the reader "to try to understand . . . how one man has tried and is trying to make a difference, despite the heavy odds against him. More than all-knowing criticism from afar, he needs prayers."--p. 10.

281.   Preface to *Washington, D.C. to Washington Square*, by John Brademas. New York: Weidenfeld and Nicolson, 1986.

282.   Foreword to *The Emerging Parish: The Notre Dame Study of Catholic Parish Life Since Vatican II*, by Jim Castelli and Joseph Gremillion. New York: Harper and Row, 1987.

"Through this study, we convey Notre Dame's admiration for and gratitude to the pastors, staffs, and lay leaders of the 19,500 parishes which comprise the

185 dioceses of the Catholic church, USA serving
regularly over 52 million faithful. We particularly
thank the thousands of parishioners and staff who
have cooperated with Notre Dame in making the study."
--p. ix.

283. Foreword to *The Guarded Gate: The Reality of American
      Refugee Policy*, by Norman L. Zucker and Naomi Flink
      Zucker. New York: Harcourt Brace Jovanovich, 1987.

      "*The Guarded Gate* details just how unjust and
      inequitable the application of the Refugee Act of 1980
      has been. It considers the harmful ramifications of
      the government's narrow interpretation of U.S. laws
      that govern asylum; . . . of long term detention of
      asylum applicants; . . . and of the arrest and forcible
      return to their countries of tens of thousands of
      desperate Central Americans seeking protection here."
      --p. x.

284. Foreword to *Revolution from the Heart*, by Niall
      O'Brien. New York: Oxford University Press, 1987.

      Hesburgh commends the efforts of the author, a
      missionary assigned to the Philippine island of
      Negros, to remedy injustice.

285. Foreword to *Courage in Mission: Presidential
      Leadership in the Church-related College*, edited by
      Duane H. Dagley. Washington, D.C.: Council for
      Advancement and Support of Education, 1988.

286. Foreword to *Multinational Managers and Host Govern-
      ment Interactions*, edited by Lee A. Tavis. Notre
      Dame, Ind.: University of Notre Dame Press, 1988.

      "I am still more than convinced that the multinational
      corporation, properly run and properly oriented, can be
      a greater engine of development than most governments."
      --p. ix.

287. Foreword to *Reflections in the Dome: Sixty Years
of Life at Notre Dame*, edited by James S. O'Rourke IV.
2d ed. Notre Dame, Ind.: James S. O'Rourke IV, 1988.

"The contributors have done what poets do--recall
emotion in tranquillity--and in their personal
accounts we catch rewarding glimses of the elusive
Notre Dame."--p. 2.

288. Foreword to *Rekindling Development: Multinational
Firms and World Debt*, edited by Lee A. Tavis.
Notre Dame, Ind.: University of Notre Dame Press,
1988.

As an overture to a work which deals with the immense
debt overhang in the Third World and stalled development, Hesburgh shares his ideas on the Third World
debt.

Newspaper Articles
by Theodore M. Hesburgh

1950-1959

289. "What Prayer Did For Me." *Chicago American*, Late edition, 1 March 1959. UNDA: UDIS-Biographical Files.

    Prayer provides wisdom and courage.

1960-1969

290. "The True Source of Human Rights." *Catholic Reporter*, 22 April 1960, p. 7.

291. "Catholic Higher Education as Mediator." *Catholic Messenger* (Davenport, Iowa), 24 August 1961, pp. 5-6.

    Excerpts from address entitled "Catholic Higher Education in Twentieth Century America," delivered at the 58th annual convention of the National Catholic Educational Association, Atlantic City, New Jersey, 4 April 1961.

292. "You Must Decide Life's Rewards." *Chicago American*, 23 May 1964. UNDA: UDIS-Biographical Files.

Substituting for vacationing Stanley Pieza, *Chicago American's* religion editor, Hesburgh suggests some enduring values that make life meaningful: commitment to truth, a passion for justice, and faith.

1970-1979

293.   "The Need for Great Teaching." *Minneapolis Star*, 20 October 1970.

"... the university must remain politically neutral as an institution, although its faculty, students, and administration are free to take their own political stance, indeed must do so when faced with national and international crises with deep moral undertones."

294.   "A Proposal for Mideast Peace . . . ." *New York Times*, 1 October 1970, p. C41.

295.   "Universities at the Crossroads." *New York Times*, 17 October 1970.

Excerpts from an address to the University of Notre Dame faculty.

296.   "Meditation on the Beginning of a New School Year." *New York Times*, 15 September 1971.

Hesburgh points out the President's opposition to busing and the core of the issue: provision of a good education for minorities. Reprinted in *Scholastic*, vol. 113, October 1, 1971, p. 25.

297.   "A Concerned Catholic." *New York Times* 30 April 1972, sec. 12 (supplement), p. 11.

Hesburgh discusses aspects of the global population problem, emphasizing the importance of human dignity. "If population growth is viewed alone as *the* one

great crisis, then we will descend to all kinds of
pragmatic and immoral initiatives. One of the most
blatant of these is abortion as a means of population
control . . . ." Reprinted in *Origins,* vol. 2
(June 8, 1972), p. 42 ff.

298.   "Father Hesburgh's Program for Racial Justice." *New
York Times Magazine,* 29 October 1972, sec. 6, 20ff.

Hesburgh discusses in depth the stark realities of
racial injustice, segregation, education, integration,
housing, employment, and other civil rights issues.
Based on a speech at Union Theological Seminary upon
receiving the Reinhold Niebuhr Award. Reprinted under
title "Human Rights: An Unfinished Business" in *Notre
Dame Magazine,* vol. 2, February 1973, pp. 40-47; and
in *Counseling and Values,* vol. 18, Spring 1974, pp.
146-53.

299.   "Even Good People Are Losing Heart." *New York Times,*
17 March 1973, p. 31.

300.   "Hesburgh Outlines Next Christian Era." *National
Catholic Reporter,* 14 December 1973.

301.   "The Hucksters." *New York Times,* 23 May 1973, p. 47.

Hesburgh analyzes the tangled web of Watergate. Among
many other contributing factors, he observes that "as a
people, we grew slack in our own personal moral commitment in so many of the ordinary aspects of personal
life, increasingly blunting our total moral sensitivity
as a nation." Reprinted as "Watergate and Our Moral
Malaise" in *Current,* vol. 153, July/August, 1973,
pp. 18-19.

302.   "What Lies Ahead for the Church? Educator Sees Many
Great Trials, But Many Signs of Hope for the Future."
Our Sunday Visitor, 9 June 1974.

Hesburgh predicts for the Church in the future
openness, moral credibility, political action, and
better leadership. "We can and must do something
about abortion . . . . It must not be booked as a
Catholic problem either; it is a human problem."
--p. 14.

303.   "A Declaration of Independence: Most of Mom's
       Problems Need Global Solutions." *National Observer,*
       7 June 1975.

304.   "Freedom and Justice Not Dead Ashes But Living Flame
       to Be Fed." *South Bend Tribune,* 6 July 1976, p. 15.

       "If we can achieve freedom and justice for all here,
       then maybe there is hope for the rest of the world."

305.   "No Strings Attached." *New York Times,* 4 February
       1976.

       Ambassador Daniel P. Moynihan's departure from the
       U.N. provides an opportunity to re-examine a basic
       issue: "Should the United States determine its
       foreign policies on the basis of whether they are
       right and just, rather than merely politically
       expedient?"

306.   "Helping the Developing Nations to Help Themselves."
       New York Times, 24 March 1979, p. 19.

307.   "Nuclear Energy and the Future." *New York Times,*
       Sunday, 14 October 1979, sec. 4, p. E18.

                        1980-1988

308.   "For the President-Elect." *New York Times,* Sunday,
       30 November 1980, sec. 7, p. 9.

Hesburgh, one of fifteen Americans interested in
policy matters, recommends books to Ronald Reagan.

309. "Humanity Is the Tie That Binds, and It Works." *Our
Sunday Visitor*, 21 December 1980.

310. "It's Time We Stop Saying 'Let the Government Do
It.'" *Our Sunday Visitor Magazine*, 8 June 1980.

311. "View From the Top: Keep Sports' Priorities in
Order." *New York Times*, Sunday, 20 December 1981, S5.

Address given at the 62nd annual football banquet,
December 10, 1981, at Notre Dame. Hesburgh restates
the University's philosophy of athletics. Reprinted
in *Notre Dame Report*, vol. 8, 1982, pp. 225-27.

312. "Voluntarism, Not Government, Is the Nation's
Backbone." *Visitor*, 12 July 1981.

313. "Why I Am Pro-Life: A Social Justice Perspective."
Visitor, 18 January 1981.

Hesburgh discusses the issue of abortion.

314. "Nothing Totalitarian About a Worker's ID Card."
New York Times, 24 September 1982, Late edition,
p. A26.

Hesburgh objects to William Safire's column "The
Computer Tattoo" (9 September). He asserts that the
U.S. needs to "legalize a substantial number of
undocumented persons currently in our country."

315. "Appraising the Draft." *National Catholic Reporter*,
22 April 1983, p. 9.

316. Letter to Ann Landers Responding to Lost Sheep.
South Bend Tribune, 3 July 1983.

Hesburgh responds to a reader's inquiry regarding abortion and excommunication.

317. "Peace, War Complicated Moral Issue." *National Catholic Reporter*, 22 April 1983, p. 8.

Hesburgh discusses his reactions to the third draft of the bishops' letter on war and peace which he considers "the finest document ever to emerge from the American hierarchy . . . ."--p. 8.

318. "Letter." *South Bend Tribune*, 26 May 1985.

By invitation from Ann Landers, Hesburgh replies to "Saving My Cyanide Pills in Greenwich."

319. "Controlling the Borders: The Worst Approach to Immigration Reform Is to Do Nothing." *Los Angeles Daily Journal*, 31 March 1986, p. 4.

320. "Dooley's Short Life Was Filled With Helping Others." *Observer*, 31 January 1986, p. 7.

321. "Enough Delay on Immigration." *New York Times*, 20 March 1986, Late edition, p. A27.

Hesburgh urges Congress to enact immigration reform now in order to continue our tradition of sharing our way of life with new immigrants. "Failure to act quickly and responsibly to control the flow of illegal immigrants to this country will inevitably lead to a quasi-military solution none of us wants."--p. A27.

322. "The Joys of Priesthood." *New York Daily News*, 17 May 1987.

At Ann Landers' request, Hesburgh responds to a letter from a concerned teenager whose brother wants to become a priest.

323. "My Faith in the Young." *The Tablet*, 7 November 1987.

In the younger generation, Hesburgh discerns among
the best a more committed Catholic equipped to create
a better and more authentic Church.

324. "Why Higher Education Isn't Making the Grade." *Los
Angeles Times*, 5 April 1987, sec. 5, p. 3.

Hesburgh discusses the problem of poor quality in
education. "The quality issue is inevitably linked
to numbers and selectivity. The greater the number
of students and the lower the criteria for admission,
the greater the quality-control problem."

Interviews With Theodore M. Hesburgh

1960-1969

325. "Notre Dame's Father Hesburgh: A New Kind of Sixty-Minute Man Leads a Great University." *Look* 25 (24 October 1961): 116-24.

    Interview with Gereon Zimmermann.

326. "Hesburgh on Civil Rights." *Scholastic* 103 (18 May 1962): 14.

    Hesburgh responds to questions by *Scholastic* reporter Ken Arnold on the civil rights situation.

327. "Father Hesburgh on: SUMMA, Religion on Campus, and His Role as President." *Scholastic* 109 (23 February 1968): 18-19.

    Part two of an interview with *Scholastic* editors. Discusses the SUMMA fund drive and investigation into institutional cooperation with St. Mary's College.

328. "Father Hesburgh on: the Dow Protest, the Kennan Article, Student Activism, and ROTC." *Scholastic* 109 (16 February 1968): 20-21.

Part one of an interview with *Scholastic* editors Mike
McInerney, Robert Metz, and John Melsheimer. Hesburgh
lays down the ground rules relevant to student
protest.

329. "Teacher I'll Never Forget." *Parent's Magazine* 43
(December 1968): 51.

Interviewed by Nick Seitz, Hesburgh commends Sister
Justina, his geometry teacher at Most Holy Rosary
High School, Syracuse, New York.

330. "Universities Run Selves, or Somebody Else Will."
Catholic Transcript, 16 May 1969.

Interview on campus unrest.

1970-1979

331. "Father Hesburgh Talks About Youth." *Anchorage News*,
23 July 1970.

Interview with Hesburgh in Alaska on student unrest,
student radicals, racism, and the draft.

332. "College Presidents and Students." *Mademoiselle* 73
(August 1971): 244ff.

333. "Notre Dame's New Breed." *Notre Dame Alumnus* 49
(August 1971): 15-19.

Edited version of a conversation with Frank Reynolds
on American Broadcasting Company's "Directions."

334. "Plan for Cooling Violence." *Today's Health* 50
(November 1972): 31-36ff.

Interview edited by F. Katz.

Valentine no. 5811.

335. "Father Theodore Hesburgh Has Just Begun to Fight New Battles of Higher Education." *College and University Business* 54 (June 1973): 29-32.

336. "An Interview With Father Hesburgh: Recollections of the Last Decade By One of Its Principal Movers and Shakers." *Civil Rights Digest* 5 (Summer 1973): 42-48.

Excerpts from an interview in 1971 by Paige Mulholland for the archives of the Lyndon Baines Johnson Library, Austin, Texas.

337. "The Priest and the President." *Notre Dame Magazine* 2 (April 1973): 45-47.

Hesburgh discusses civil rights issues and President Johnson's request for a special study on racial imbalance in public schools.

338. "An Interview with Father Theodore M. Hesburgh on Higher Education in Transition." *Today's Education* 63 (November-December 1974): 58-62.

Interview by Harold G. Shane, Professor of Education, Indiana University, Bloomington. Surveys the field of postsecondary education.

339. "Thin Edge of Starvation." *A.D. Correspondence* 9 (28 September 1974): 2-7.

Interview with Hesburgh on his work with the Overseas Development Council, and the problems of global starvation.

340. "Notre Dame's Father Hesburgh." *Change* 8 (February 1976): 46-51ff.

Interview by Gary MacEoin.

341. "Revival Tents and Golden Domes." *U.S. Catholic* 41
      (March 1976): 6-14.

      Edward Wakin interviews Rev. Billy Graham and
      Hesburgh. The distinctive styles of the two
      religious leaders emerge.

342. "Father Theodore Hesburgh Is Notre Dame's Most
      Durable Triple Threat: President, Priest and
      Activist." *People* 8 (26 September 1977): 70-77.

      Interview by Linda Witt. Includes portrait of Hesburgh,
      about age 7, with his mother and his sisters Betty
      and Mary.

343. "Hesburgh: Dean of Presidents." *Scholastic* 118
      (2 May 1977): 4-7.

      Interview by Kathleen McElroy and Thomas Kruczek.
      Hesburgh discusses major decisions he has made as
      president of Notre Dame, and as a public figure in the
      areas of religion, education, and social policy.

344. "An Interview With Father Hesburgh." *Notre Dame
      Magazine* 6 (June 1977): 22-27.

      Interview by Rev. John L. Reedy, C.S.C., on the Catholic
      character of the university, holding public elective
      office, management style, and close friendships.

345. "What Has Pleased You Most About Those 25 Years?"
      South Bend Tribune: Michiana Section, 19 June 1977.

      Interview with Gerald Lutkus.

346. "How to Hesburgh a Country's Conscience." *U.S.
      Catholic* 44 (May 1979): 25-30.

Interview with Dennis Geaney.

347.   "A Visitor Interview: Father Theodore Hesburgh," by
       Catherine Anthony. Photos by John Zierten. *Visitor*,
       2 December 1979.

                        1980-1988

348.   "People Feel the Entire Immigration System Is Out of
       Control." *U.S. News and World Report* 89 (13 October
       1980): 63-64.

349.   "Interview with Hesburgh." *Hope College Anchor*,
       Holland, Michigan, 10 September 1981, p. 3.

       The future of public and private colleges, racism,
       and the South African situation are among the topics
       discussed in an interview with Anne Brown.

350.   "Theodore Hesburgh: Leader of the Fighting Irish."
       Geo: the Earth Diary, (January 1982): 9-16.

       Interview by Robert Sam Anson.

351.   "Where We Agree On God." Dialogue between Martin E.
       Marty and T. M. Hesburgh. *50 Plus* 23 (December 1983):
       16-21.

352.   "Hesburgh of Notre Dame: The Renowned Educator-
       Humanitarian Calls Himself a 'Utility Infielder.'"
       Dynamic Years 19 (March-April 1984): 26-29.

       Interview by Annette Winter.

353.   Interview with Dr. Dean Porter, Snite Museum of Art,
       University of Notre Dame, on the origin of Ivan
       Mestrovic's *Christ and the Samaritan Woman at Jacob's
       Well.* In *Treasures of the Vatican: New Orleans
       Vatican Pavilion at the 1984 Louisiana World*

Exposition: Jesus Christ Our Redeemer in Art: Ages, Images, Impact, edited by Val A. McInnes, 34-36. New Orleans: New Orleans Vatican Pavilion, 1984.

Hesburgh explains the origin of a work by Ivan Mestrovic, internationally renowned Yugoslavian sculptor, who brought forth his celebrated bronze sculpture, *Christ and the Samaritan Woman at Jacob's Well* in 1957. Specially recast from the Snite Museum Collection, this work served as the centerpiece of the Vatican Pavilion at the New Orleans Fair, 1984.

354. "A Catholic Education, A Force in America." *University of Waterloo Courier* (June 1985): 9-16.

Interviewed by Rob Donelson, St. Jerome's College. Hesburgh responds to questions concerning priests involved in politics, relationships with American presidents, and the role of women in the Church.

355. "In Spite of Everything." In *Against Silence: The Voice and Vision of Elie Wiesel,* selected and edited by Irving Abrahamson, vol. 3, 259-63. New York: Holocaust Library, 1985.

Adapted from an interview with Frank Reynolds, American Broadcasting Company, *Directions,* ABC TV, 18 June 1978. Hesburgh calls the Holocaust "the ultimate of blasphemies." Wiesel and Hesburgh share in their experience of the memory of the past, the faith of the present, and hope for the future.

356. "Father Hesburgh Offers Balance: Notre Dame President Speaks on South Africa, Free Speech, Academic Concerns, College Athletics, and Politics." *Dartmouth Review* (16 April 1986): 8-9.

Interview by Chris Whitman. Hesburgh asserts that the heart of the divestment issue is not apartheid, but pragmatic judgment.

357. "On Catholic College Boards,'Lay People Thank God.'"
     New York Times, 16 November 1986, Late edition, p.
     E24.

     Interview by A. E. Hardie on changes in governance of
     Catholic colleges and universities.

358. "Theodore M. Hesburgh, C.S.C." In *What Works for Me:
     16 CEOs Talk About Their Careers and Commitments,* by
     Thomas R. Horton, 151-77. New York: Random House
     Business Division, 1986.

     Hesburgh describes his administrative style in crisis
     management, delegation, working with boards of
     directors and trustees, and other areas.

359. "Father Theodore M. Hesburgh. Interviewed by Lois
     Ferm. March 25, 1987." Billy Graham Oral History
     Program: O.H. 795. 18 pp. 1987. Photocopy of
     typescript. UNDA.

     Hesburgh discusses the Billy Graham Crusade held at
     Notre Dame in 1977.

360. "Father Theodore Hesburgh's Personal Campaign." *Our
     Sunday Visitor,* 7 June 1987.

     In part 1 of an interview with Catherine M. Odell,
     Hesburgh states he is most satisfied with the transfer
     of governance to lay control, and with coeducation.
     He considers the University more Catholic since it
     has come under lay control. Notre Dame's first
     priority, evident in both the Committee on University
     Priorities (COUP) and the Priorities and Commitments
     to Excellence (PACE) reports, focuses on the process
     of becoming a great Catholic university.

361. "Father Theodore M. Hesburgh: an OSV Interview." *Our
     Sunday Visitor,* 14 June 1987.

In part 2 of an interview by Catherine M. Odell,
Hesburgh discusses the Vatican document on higher
education and the commitment to academic freedom.
Hesburgh believes *The Catholic University in the
Modern World*, issued by the International Federation
of Catholic Universities, "perfectly balanced the
concerns of the Church and of the Catholic university
to be themselves."

362. "Father Theodore Hesburgh: Notre Dame's President
Steps Down." *St. Anthony Messenger* 94 (May 1987): 28-
34.

Extensive interview by Catherine Walsh on Hesburgh's
career.

363. "T. M. Hesburgh: An Educator, Statesman and Priest
Celebrates 35 Years of Impact." *CGA World: The
Official Magazine of Catholic Golden Age* 7 (Fall,
1987): 20-25.

Interview with Lorraine Sherbine. Focuses on three
spheres of Hesburgh's life: academic, religious, and
government service. Hesburgh offers his comments on
several U.S. presidents.

364. "Theodore Hesburgh." In *Top Guns: Seventeen World
Leaders in Politics, Media and Business Tell How They
Made It to the Top--and Stayed There.* South
Melbourne: Sun Books, Macmillan Company of Australia,
1988.

In an extensive interview, Hesburgh responds to
questions regarding his extraordinarily successful
career, his physical and intellectual momentum, his
leadership roles in government, his views of the
Church, authority, and a variety of other issues.

Government Documents

1950-1959

365. "Statement by Commissioner Theodore M. Hesburgh." In U.S. Commission on Civil Rights. . . . *One Nation Under God, Indivisible, With Liberty and Justice for All*, 195-99. Washington, D.C.: GPO, 1959.

An abridgment of the Report of the United States Commission on Civil Rights. Hesburgh explicates issues of desegregation and housing.

SuDoc no. CR1.1:959.

1970-1979

366. Statement by Rev. T. M. Hesburgh. In U.S. Congress. House. Committee on Banking and Currency. Subcommittee on Housing. *Housing and Urban Development Legislation, 1971.* Part 3. Hearings. 92nd Cong., 1st sess., 1099-1130. Washington, D.C.: GPO, 1971.

SuDoc no. Y4.B22/1:H81/46/971/pt. 3.

367. Statement by Rev. T. M. Hesburgh. In U.S. Congress. Senate. Committee on Labor and Public Welfare.

122   Theodore M. Hesburgh

Subcommittee on Labor. *Equal Employment Opportunities Enforcement Act of 1971.* Hearings. 92nd Cong., 1st sess., 195-201. Washington, D.C.: GPO, 1971.

SuDoc no. Y4.L11/2:Em7/16/971.

368. Statement by Rev. T. M. Hesburgh. In U.S. Congress. Senate. Committee on the Judiciary. Subcommittee on Administrative Practice and Procedure. *Presidential Commissions.* Hearings. 92nd Cong., 1st sess., 229-86. Washington, D.C.: GPO, 1971.

SuDoc no. Y4.J89/2:P92/13.

369. Statement by Rev. T. M. Hesburgh. In U.S. Congress. House. Committee on Education and Labor. *Equal Educational Opportunities Act.* Part 3. Hearings. 92nd Cong., 2d sess., 1416-56. Washington, D.C.: GPO, 1972.

SuDoc no. Y4.Ed8/1:Ed8/41/pt.3.

370. Statement by Rev. T. M. Hesburgh. In U.S. Congress. House. Committee on the Judiciary. Subcommittee No. 5. *School Busing.* Part 1. Hearings. 92nd Cong., 2d sess., 184-243. Washington, D.C.: GPO, 1972.

SuDoc no. Y4.J89/1:92-32/pt. 1.

371. Statement of Rev. T. M. Hesburgh. In U.S. Congress. Senate. Committee on the Judiciary. Subcommittee on Constitutional Rights. *Civil Rights Commission.* Hearing. 92nd Cong., 2d sess., 10-28. Washington, D.C.: GPO, 1972.

Testimony on S.3121 and H.R. 12652, legislation to extend the life of the Commission, expand its jurisdiction to include sex discrimination, and to authorize appropriations for the Commission.

SuDoc no. Y4.J89/2:C49/10/972.

372. Statement by Rev. T. M. Hesburgh. In U.S. Congress.
House. Committee on Foreign Affairs. Subcommittee on
International Organizations and Movements.
*International Protection of Human Rights: The Work of
International Organizations and the Role of U.S.
Foreign Policy.* Hearings. 93d Cong., 1st sess., 319-
35. Washington, D.C.: GPO, 1973.

SuDoc no. Y4.F76/1:H88/4.

373. Statement by Rev. T. M. Hesburgh. In U.S. Congress.
Senate. Committee on Foreign Relations. *Foreign
Economic Assistance. 1973.* Hearings. 93d Cong., 1st
sess., 262-72. Washington, D.C.: GPO, 1973.

SuDoc no. Y4.F76/2:Ec7/4/973.

374. Statement by Rev. T. M. Hesburgh. In U.S. Congress.
House. Committee on the Judiciary. Subcommittee on
Civil and Constitutional Rights. *Extension of the
Voting Rights Act.* Part 1. Hearings. 94th Cong., 1st
sess., 320-57. Washington, D.C.: GPO, 1975.

SuDoc no. Y4.J89/1:94-1/pt. 1.

375. Statement of Rev. T. M. Hesburgh. In U.S. Congress.
Senate. Committee on Commerce, Science, and
Transportation. Subcommittee on Science, Technology,
and Space. *U.S. Preparation for the 1979 U.N.
Conference on Science and Technology for Develop-
ment.* Hearing. 95th Cong., 1st sess., 3-30.
Washington, D.C.: GPO, 1977.

Statements of Lucy Wilson Benson, Hesburgh, and Jean
M. Wilkowski on the background and purposes of the
1979 Conference, the U.S. objectives at the Conference, and the current state of U.S. preparations.

124　Theodore M. Hesburgh

SuDoc no. Y4.C73/7:95-59.

376. "Closing Statement by Ambassador Hesburgh." In *U.N. Conference: U.S. Statements On Science & Technology, August 20-31, 1979*, 5-6. Current Policy no. 88. Washington, D.C.: U.S. Dept. of State, Bureau of Public Affairs, Office of Public Communication, Editorial Division, 1979.

SuDoc no. S1. 71/4:88.

377. *Emergency Aid in Kampuchean Crisis*, 2. Current Policy no. 100. Washington, D.C.: Dept. of State, Bureau of Public Affairs, 1979.

Includes Carter's announcement of assistance for victims of Kampuchean crisis and press briefing by Hesburgh, Ambassador Henry Owen, and leaders of the private sector.

SuDoc no. S1.71/4:100.

378. "Opening Address by Ambassador Hesburgh." In *U.N. Conference: U.S. Statements On Science & Technology, August 20-31, 1979*, 2-5. Current Policy no. 88. Washington, D.C.: U.S. Dept. of State, Bureau of Public Affairs, Office of Public Communication, Editorial Division, 1979.

SuDoc no. S1.71/4:88.

379. "Relief Efforts." Current Policy no. 111. Washington, D.C.: Dept. of State, Bureau of Public Affairs, 1979.

Remarks by President Carter, Hesburgh, and Mrs. Carter on relief efforts for Kampuchean refugees, 13 November 1979.

SuDoc no. S1.71/4:111.

380. "Science and Technology: U.N. Conference on Science
      and Technology for Development." In U.S. Dept. of
      State. *Department of State Bulletin* 79 (November
      1979): 51-54.

      Remarks at the opening and closing sessions of the
      U.N. Conference on Science and Technology held in
      Vienna, 20-31 August 1979. Hesburgh, chairman of
      the U.S. delegation, concludes that the conference
      "has reached agreement on a program of action to
      enhance scientific and technological capacity in the
      developing countries and to improve international
      information flows and the commercial transfer of
      science and technology."--p. 54.

      SuDoc no. S1.3.

381. Statement by Rev. T. M. Hesburgh. In U.S. Congress.
      House. Committee on Science and Technology. *Joint
      Seminars on the U.N. Conference on Science and
      Technology for Development (UNCSTD)*. Joint Hearings.
      96th Cong., 1st sess., 76-85. Washington, D.C.: GPO,
      1979.

      SuDoc no. Y4.Sci2:96/13.

382. Statement by Rev. T. M. Hesburgh. In U.S. Congress.
      Senate. Committee on Commerce, Science, and Trans-
      portation. Subcommittee on Science, Technology,
      and Space. *U.S. Policies and Initiatives for the U.N.
      Conference on Science and Technology for Development.*
      Joint Hearing. 96th Cong., 1st sess., 14-16.
      Washington, D.C.: GPO, 1979.

      SuDoc no. Y4.C73/7:96-43.

383. Statement by Rev. T. M. Hesburgh. In U.S. Congress.
      Senate. Committee on Foreign Relations. *International*

Development Assistance Act of 1979. Hearings. 96th
Cong., 1st sess., 167-71. Washington, D.C.: GPO,
1979.

SuDoc no. Y4.F76/2:In8/52/979.

384.   United Nations. Conference on Science and Technology
for Development. Vienna, 1979. *Report of the United
Nations Conference on Science and Technology for
Development, Vienna (20-31 August 1979)*. New York:
United Nations, 1979.

(Document - United Nations); A/CONF. 81/16.

1980-1988

385.   "Mrs. Carter Visits Thailand." *Department of State
Bulletin* 80, no. 2034 (January 1980): 5-7.

Reports of Carter, Hesburgh, and Mrs. Carter on the
refugee crisis in Thailand. Hesburgh summarizes
results of consultation to exchange information on
the situation in Thailand and Cambodia.

SuDoc no. S1.3:80/2034.

386.   *Second Semiannual Report to Congress*. U.S. Select
Commission on Immigration and Refugee Policy.
Washington, D.C.: GPO, 1980.

Includes Hesburgh's "Letter of Transmittal" dated
1 September 1980 to the Congress. "To these goals
the Select Commission dedicates its task: The
reunification of families, the playing of a
responsible role in the world, the strengthening
of our country, the reform of our laws to make them
clear and equitable, and their firm, steady
enforcement."--p. vi.

SuDoc no. Y4.J 89/1:Im 6/9.

387. *Semiannual Report to Congress.* U.S. Select Commission
on Immigration and Refugee Policy. Washington, D.C.:
GPO, 1980.

The first semiannual report, dated March 1980,
outlines efforts of the Commission, chaired by
Hesburgh, to review U.S. immigration laws and
policies. The report describes the Commission's
mandate, the issues to be examined, and reviews highlights of the first six months' work.

SuDoc no. Y4. J 89/2:Im 7/3.

388. Statement by Rev. T. M. Hesburgh. In U.S. Congress.
House. Committee on Appropriations. Subcommittee on
Departments of State, Justice, Commerce, the
Judiciary, and Related Agencies Appropriations.
*Departments of State, Justice, and Commerce, the
Judiciary, and Related Agencies Appropriations for
1981.* Part 8. Hearings. 96th Cong., 2d sess., 748-
59. Washington, D.C.: GPO, 1980.

SuDoc no. Y4.Ap6/1:St2/981/pt.8.

389. Statement by Rev. T. M. Hesburgh. In U.S. Congress.
Senate. Committee on Appropriations. Subcommittee on
Departments of State, Justice, and Commerce, the
Judiciary, and Related Agencies. *Departments of
State, Justice, and Commerce, the Judiciary, and
Related Agencies Appropriations for Fiscal Year 1981.*
Part 1. Hearings. 96th Cong., 2d sess., 15-50.
Washington, D.C.: GPO, 1980.

SuDoc no. Y4.Ap6/2:St2/981/pt.1.

390. "Views From the Top." *Synergist* 9 (Spring 1980): 19-
20.

128   Theodore M. Hesburgh

Hesburgh stresses the need for lifelong service to
one's neighbor.

SuDoc no. AA3.9:9/1.

391. U.S. Select Commission on Immigration and Refugee
      Policy. *U.S. Immigration Policy and the National
      Interest: Final Report and Recommendations* . . . with
      supplemental views by commissioners, 1 March 1981.
      Washington, D.C.: The Select Commission, 1981.

      As chairman of the Commission on Immigration and
      Refugee Policy, Hesburgh summarizes the Commission's
      recommendations: "We recommend closing the back
      door to undocumented/illegal migration, opening the
      front door a little more to accommodate legal
      migration in the interests of this country, defining
      our immigration goals clearly and providing a
      structure to implement them effectively, and setting
      forth procedures which will lead to fair and
      efficient adjudication and administration of U.S.
      immigration laws."--p. 3.

      Includes Hesburgh's "Letter of Transmittal," dated
      1 March 1981, to President Ronald W. Reagan (p. v.);
      Hesburgh's "Introduction to the Final Report of the
      Select Commission on Immigration and Refugee Policy,"
      (pp. 1-17); and "Statement of Chairman Theodore M.
      Hesburgh" (Appendix B: pp. 333-39).

      SuDoc no. Y 3.Im 6/2:2 Im 6/981.

392. U.S. Select Commission on Immigration and Refugee
      Policy. *U.S. Immigration Policy and the National
      Interest: Staff Report* . . . 30 April 1981.
      Washington, D.C.: The Select Commission, 1981.
      10 vols.

      "This staff report and its accompanying appendixes
      provide additional background data and analysis to

the recommendations made by the Select Commission on
Immigration and Refugee Policy in its final report on
March 1, 1981. This report also presents an outline
of strategies and programs to implement several of
the major recommendations made by Select Commission-
ers."--p. ix. The last section includes an extensive
selected bibliography compiled by Sheila H. Murphy
and Philip M. Wharton on topics of particular interest
to researchers (pp. 801-916).

Nine appendix volumes include: Appendix A: *Papers
on U.S. Immigration History*; Appendix B: *Papers on
International Migration*; Appendix C: *Papers on
Refugees*; Appendix D: *Papers on Legal Immigration to
the United States*; Appendix E: *Papers on Illegal
Migration to the United States*; Appendix F: *Papers
on Temporary Workers*; Appendix G: *Papers on the
Administration of Immigration Law*; Appendix H:
Public Information Supplement, consisting of "Public
Hearings--Revised Agendas and Summaries," pp. 9-245;
*Select Commission on Immigration and Refugee Policy
Newsletter* (1979-1981), pp. 551-661; "Selected
Editorials and Articles," pp. 663-701; and Appendix
I: Summary of Commission Recommendations and Votes,
which contains Hesburgh's "Introduction to the Final
Report on the Select Commission on Immigration and
Refugee Policy," pp. 8-24.

"Supplement to the Final Report and recommendations
of the Select Commission on Immigration and Refugee
Policy."

SuDoc no. Y 3.Im 6/2:2 Im 6/2:2Im 6/staff.
SuDoc no. Y 3.Im 6/2:2 Im 6/981 staff/app. A-I.

Non-Print Materials

1960-1969

393. "Convocation Address. Valparaiso University,
Valparaiso, Indiana, November 1, 1967." Valparaiso,
Ind.: University Archives, 1967. Sound cassette.
UNDA.

Hesburgh discusses the Catholic view of Martin Luther.

1970-1979

394. *CBS News Special Report: Issue of Busing.* Produced
by CBS News; executive director: Ernest Leiser; news
correspondent, Roger Mudd. New York: CBS Television
Network, 1972. Videorecording. 2 reels. 16 mm.

Telecast of 30 April 1972.
"A television special in which nine speakers, Rep.
John Conyers, Sen. John Tower, former Congressman
Norman Lent, Father Theodore Hesburgh of Notre Dame
University, Roy Wilkins of the NAACP, HEW Secretary
Elliot Richardson, Roy Innis of CORE, Attorney
General Richard Kleindienst, and former Supreme
Court Justice Arthur Goldberg present opposing views
on the issue of busing for racial integration of the
public schools of the United States. Includes

excerpts of speeches by President Richard Nixon
. . . ." OCLC no. 14965117.

395. Commencement Address, Stonehill College, North
      Easton, Massachusetts: May, 1972. North Easton,
      Mass: Stonehill College Archives, 1972. Sound
      cassette. UNDA.

      On change, compassion, commitment, and eternal life.

396. *A Question of Survival* by Theodore Hesburgh, Mark
      Tannenbaum, and Arthur Simon. Vital History Cassettes.
      New York: Encyclopedia Americana, CBS News Audio
      Resource Library, 1974. Sound cassette. Duration:
      26 min.

      Discussion of hunger, starvation, and food relief.

397. *U.S. Self-Interest and International Moral
      Imperative.* Santa Barbara, Calif.: Center for
      the Study of Democratic Institutions, 1974. Sound
      cassette. Duration: 27 min.

      Recorded at the third Pacem in Terris Convocation,
      Washington, D.C., 1973, sponsored by the Center for
      the Study of Democratic Institutions. Hesburgh
      "challenges America to combine a sense of national
      self-restraint with respect for the needs of other
      countries. 'We must not sustain affluence in the
      United States at the expense of human development
      elsewhere.'"

398. *Openness in the Church.* Kansas City: National
      Catholic Reporter, 1976. Sound cassette.

      "Lecture given at the Catholic Press Association
      annual convention, Denver. Discussion of change
      in the Church since Vatican II and of expectations
      for the Church of the future."--OCLC no. 3088252.

399. *Hesburgh of Notre Dame.* Vital History Cassettes;
      June '77, no. 1. New York: Encyclopedia Americana/CBS
      News Audio Resource Library, 1977. Sound cassette.
      OCLC no. 4199397.

      Hesburgh, interviewed by Dan Rather on "Who's Who"
      on 26 June 1977, discusses his role as president
      of Notre Dame, friend and advisor to executives,
      member of corporate boards, and spokesman for civil
      rights.

400. "Phil Donahue." Videorecording. ABC-TV. Spring,
      1979. VHS. UNDA.

      Hesburgh discusses alcohol consumption on campus and
      Catholic education.

                          1980-1988

401. "Commemoration Day Ceremonies, February 22, 1980."
      The Johns Hopkins University, Baltimore, Maryland.
      Baltimore: The Ferdinand Hamburger, Jr. Archives,
      1980. Sound cassette. UNDA.

      On the 104th anniversary of the founding of the
      University, Hesburgh speaks on voluntarism, the need
      to educate students to academic excellence, and the
      importance of service to the needy.

      For printed version, see item no. 528.

402. *Theodore Hesburgh: The Future of Education.* Produced
      by Peter Mann; directed by Rose Russo. Transforma-
      tions: Renewing the Earth. New York: Sadlier Media
      Productions, 1980? Videorecording. U-matic.
      Duration: 30 min. OCLC no. 14062298.

      Hesburgh discusses values in education and the need
      for excellence in American education.

403. *Immigration Laws*. St. Paul, Minn.: MPR., 1981. Sound
      cassette. Duration: 42 min.

      Broadcast 10 April 1981. Hesburgh discusses the
      problem of aliens and immigration laws.

404. *Quality and Equality in American Education*. Reston,
      Va.: National Association of Secondary School Princi-
      pals, 1981. Videorecording. VHS. Duration: 35 min.

      At the third general session of a conference of the
      National Association of Secondary School Principals,
      23 February 1981, Atlanta, Georgia, Hesburgh
      discusses the problem of quality education and
      equality of opportunity in America. Particularly
      among minorities, Hesburgh considers conditions
      appalling. Illiteracy runs rampant. He suggests
      educational parks as a possible solution. Following
      his address, Hesburgh received the Association's
      Distinguished Service Award.

      For audio, see item no. 405. For printed version, see
      item no. 534.

405. *Quality-Equality Is Education's Major Challenge*.
      Anaheim, Calif.: National Association of Secondary
      School Principals, 1981. Sound cassette. Duration:
      30 min.

      For video, see item no. 404. For printed version, see
      item no. 534.

406. "The Role of the Liberal Arts." Address given . . . at
      the Fall Convocation opening the 1981-82 Academic
      Year, Tuesday, 1 September, Hope College, Holland,
      Michigan. Holland: Hope College, 1981. Sound
      cassette. UNDA.

      Hesburgh discusses the meaning of being truly human
      and describes those qualities which characterize a

liberally educated person.

407.   *The U.S. Immigration Debate.* Moderated by John
       Callaway. Conversations From Wingspread, R-790.
       Racine, Wis.: The Johnson Foundation, 1981. Sound
       cassette. Duration: 28 min. OCLC no. 9916130.

       "Examines aspects of current U.S. immigration policy
       and changes recommended by the Select Commission
       on Immigration and Refugee Policy." Taped 28 March
       1981.

408.   "Baccalaureate Address." Kalamazoo College,
       Kalamazoo, Michigan, 1982. Kalamazoo: Kalamazoo
       College Library, 1982. Sound cassette. UNDA.

       Explores the meaning of a Christian life.

409.   Commencement. University of Notre Dame, 1982.
       Notre Dame, Ind.: Educational Media, 1982.
       Videorecording. UNDA.

       Videorecordings of Hesburgh's participation in
       commencement and other academic exercises at the
       University of Notre Dame from 1983 to 1987 are also
       available.

410.   "Father Hesburgh's Informal Talk With Students and
       Faculty." Denver: Loretto Heights College, 1982.
       Sound cassette. UNDA.

       Hesburgh discusses the nuclear threat during Heights
       Week at Loretto Heights College on 13 October 1982.

411.   "60 Minutes." CBS News. 14 March 1982.
       Videorecording. U-Matic. UNDA.

412.   "Celibacy." Nightline-ABC-TV. 29 March 1983.
       Videorecording. VHS. UNDA.

413. "The Church and Politics in El Salvador."
     Nightline-ABC-TV. 8 March 1983. Videorecording.
     VHS. UNDA.

414. "The Holocaust." CBS News. Videorecording. 12 April
     1983. VHS. UNDA.

415. "One-On-One." ABC News interview. 24 June 1983.
     Videorecording. VHS. UNDA.

416. "Commencement Address, West Virginia Wesleyan College,
     Buckhannon, W.V., May 13, 1984." Buckhannon: West
     Virginia Wesleyan College, 1984. 2 sound cassettes.
     UNDA.

     On the meaning of life and the value of competence,
     compassion, and commitment.

417. "Nightline." ABC-TV. 13 September 1984. Video-
     recording. VHS. UNDA.

     Satellite feed before Mario Cuomo's lecture at the
     University of Notre Dame.

418. *Science, Religion, and the Nuclear Menace: An Address*
     by Theodore M. Hesburgh. ARCO forum of Public
     Affairs, 8 March 1984. Cambridge, Mass.: John F.
     Kennedy School of Government, Harvard University,
     1984. 2 videorecordings. 3/4 in. Duration: 60
     min. each. OCLC no. 10592290.

419. *Theodore Hesburgh: Catholics and Nuclear War.*
     Transformations: Renewing the Earth. Produced by Peter
     Mann; directed by Rose Russo. New York: Sadlier Media
     Productions, 1984? Videorecording. U-matic.
     Duration: 30 min. OCLC no. 14062326.

     Hesburgh discusses his efforts to unite scientific
     and religious leaders against the dangers of nuclear
     war.

420. "Palm Sunday Mass at Sacred Heart Church." NBC
     Special. 31 March 1985. U-Matic. Videorecording.
     UNDA.

421. Aquinas College. Commencement Address. 10 May 1986.
     Grand Rapids, Mich.: Aquinas College, 1986. Sound
     cassette. UNDA.

     Hesburgh stresses the need for competence, compassion
     and commitment, citing Tom Dooley, Mother Teresa,
     and Albert Schweitzer as models.

422. *A Conversation With Father Theodore Hesburgh.*
     Alan Bickley, moderator. Conversations from
     Wingspread; R-1180. Racine, Wis.: The Johnson
     Foundation, 1986. Sound cassette. Duration: 30
     min. OCLC no. 15036590.

     Hesburgh discusses his role on various commissions
     and his role as president of the University of Notre
     Dame.

423. Clarke Memorial Mass, October 1986. Notre Dame,
     Ind.: Educational Media, 1986. Videorecording.

     Hesburgh officiated at the dedication of the Clarke
     War Memorial, erected to honor alumni who died while
     serving in the armed forces since World War II. The
     memorial was a gift of the late Maude Clarke, former
     lieutenant colonel in the Army Nurse Corps, in memory
     of her husband, John W. Clarke.

424. "A Report On the Extraordinary Synod." South
     Bend, Ind.: Golden Dome Productions, 1986. Video-
     recording. Duration: 30 min.

     Hesburgh introduces a teleconference on the
     Extraordinary Synod, aired Monday, 20 January 1986,
     from the studios of WNDU-TV.

425. Baccalaureate Mass. May, 1987. Notre Dame, Ind.: Educational Media, 1987. Videorecording. UNDA.

426. Commencement Address, University of Pittsburgh, Pittsburgh, Pennsylvania, 10 May 1987. Pittsburgh: Archives, University of Pittsburgh, 1987. Sound cassette. UNDA.

   For printed version, see item no. 560.

427. "Community Celebration: A Tribute to Father Hesburgh." Notre Dame, Ind.: Educational Media, 1987. Videorecording. Duration: 93 min.

   At a celebration held in his honor on 10 March 1987 at the Century Center, South Bend, Hesburgh spoke at length about Notre Dame's involvement in community affairs. As a tribute to his many years of service, he was presented with a sculpture by Rodin.

428. Inauguration: Father Malloy. September 1987. Notre Dame, Ind.: Educational Media, 1987. Videorecording. UNDA.

429. "A Notre Dame Moment: Recorded Live, 5/9/87." South Bend, Ind.: Golden Dome Productions, 1987. Videorecording.

   Narrated by Walter Cronkite, this videorecording highlights Hesburgh's thirty-five years as priest, president, and public servant. A twelve page booklet, designed to accompany this telecast of Hesburgh's valedictory to Notre Dame students, alumni and friends on 9 May 1987 contains many photographs of Hesburgh during his career.

   For printed version of Father Hesburgh's valedictory address of 9 May 1987, see item no. 562.

Unpublished Works:
Addresses, Papers, Speeches

1940-1949

430. *The Mystical Body and the Apostolate: Notes Adapted from "Corps Mystique et Apostolat" of Chanoine P. Glorieux.* Notre Dame, Ind.: C.A.S. Editions, 194? Mimeo.

    Notes adapted from Canon Glorieux's work which treats the doctrine of the Mystical Body of Christ.

431. "The Christian Family." Feast of the Holy Family. Notre Dame, 1947. Typescript. 3 pp. UNDA

    "It would be difficult to find a more important element in life than the family, for it is in the family that life originates, develops, and fructifies. Yet in our day, there is hardly any other element of society more under fire than the family. And it is not exaggerating to say that the Christian family is fighting for its life."--p. 1.

432. *Dogma Notes.* 2 vols. Notre Dame, Ind.: Department of Religion, University of Notre Dame, 1948.

    Notes on dogma prepared for Notre Dame students in the Department of Religion. Hesburgh developed his textbook *God and the World of Man* from *Dogma Notes.*

433. "Annual Football Banquet, December 12, 1949." Carbon.
UNDA: UDIS-Biographical Files.

Examines the spirit of competition, cooperation, and
team work.

1950-1959

434. "Peace of God." Address delivered . . . at Tulane University for Religious Emphasis Week, March 1951. Typescript. 19 pp. UNDA

Hesburgh draws from St. Thomas Aquinas in defining
peace as "'tranquility of order.'" "There is very
little we can do about international peace short of
prayer, but we can do everything, with God's help,
about our own peace of soul."--p. 16.

435. "Address given . . . at the conference banquet of the
American Catholic Philosophical Association, Morris
Inn, Notre Dame, Indiana, April 7, 1953." Carbon.
UNDA: UDIS-Biographical Files.

Hesburgh discusses the function of philosophy as
mediator linking science and theology.

436. "'I live, now not I, but Christ liveth in me.--
Gal. 2:20.'" Sermon delivered at the Solemn Red Mass
of the Catholic Lawyers Guild of Chicago, Chicago
Illinois, Sunday, 1 November 1953. Photocopy. UNDA:
UDIS-Biographical Files.

Hesburgh describes in detail the life of St. Thomas
More.

437. "Liberal Education in the World Today." Address
delivered . . . at the Annual Meeting of the
Association of American Colleges, on 12 January 1955
in Washington, D.C. Carbon. UNDA: UDIS-Biographical

Files.

438. "Notre Dame Men--Father and Son." Sermon
delivered . . . on 'Church of the Air,' CBS Radio
Network, Sunday, 30 January 1955 - 10:30 AM EST.
Mimeo. UNDA: UDIS-Biographical Files.

Reflects on the lives and deaths of Fred Miller, Sr.,
all-American tackle, and his son, Fred Miller, Jr.
Both were killed on 17 December 1955 in an airplane
crash in Milwaukee.

439. "Address at . . . Notre Dame's President's Committee
Dinner." 1957? Carbon. UNDA: UDIS-Biographical Files.

Describes travels to South American countries, the
problems of science, and Atoms for Peace.

440. "Sermon delivered . . . at the dedication of Saint John
Church and Catholic Student Center, Michigan State
University, East Lansing, Michigan, Sunday Morning,
January 12, 1958." 1957. Carbon. UNDA: UDIS-
Biographical Files.

Reflects on the life and teaching of John Henry
Newman and the importance of Newman clubs at state
universities.

441. "Summary Report on the Meetings of the General
Conference of the International Atomic Energy Agency,
October 1-25, 1957, Vienna, Austria." 48 pp.
Typescript. UNDA: CPHS-IAEA.

Submitted by Hesburgh and Frank M. Folsom, Vatican
delegates. Report dated 23 October 1957.

442. "The Divine Romance of Catholic Education." Address
delivered . . . at Commencement Exercises, Villanova
University, Villanova, Pennsylvania, Monday, 2 June
1958. Carbon. UNDA: UDIS-Biographical Files.

Hesburgh sees creation, incarnation, sanctification
and glory as the deepest sources of inspiration
available to man.

443. "Report on the Second General Conference of the
International Atomic Energy Agency, Vienna, Austria,
September 22 to October 4, 1958." 11 pp. Photocopy.
UNDA: CPHS-IAEA.

444. "'That God May Be Glorified In All Things.'" Address
delivered . . . at Commencement Exercises, St. Benedict's
College, Atcheson, Kansas, Wednesday, 28 May 1958.
Carbon. UNDA: UDIS-Biographical Files.

Examines the value of Catholic education in the
context of the Benedictine tradition.

445. "Theology in the University. Delivered at Johns
Hopkins 19 March 1958." Carbon. UNDA: UDIS-
Biographical Files.

Quotes at length John Henry Newman and Dr. Edward B.
Pusey on the importance of theology as a proper
subject in the university curriculum.

446. "Concluding Supplementary Statement of Father
Hesburgh." 1959. 4 pp. Photocopy. UNDA.

Valentine no. 6839.

Hesburgh states that civil rights are corollaries
of the proposition that every individual is a
res sacra, a sacred reality.

447. "Opening Statement of Father Hesburgh." Hearing on
Housing, Federal Building, Chicago, Illinois, 5 May
1959. 5 pp. Photocopy. UNDA.

Valentine no. 6820.

1960-1969

448. "The Value of Life." Commencement Exercises,
University of Rhode Island, Kingston, Rhode Island,
Monday, 13 June 1960. Kingston, R.I.: University of
Rhode Island, 1960. Photocopy. UNDA.

Articulates the values of truth, beauty, justice,
dedication, sacrifice, commitment to excellence, and
respect for spiritual realities.

449. "Address given . . . at the Alumni Federation of Columbia
University Commencement Luncheon, Tuesday, June 6,
1961." Carbon. UNDA: UDIS-Biographical Files.
Issued as press release, Columbia University, under
the title "The Modern Alumnus."

Hesburgh assumes the modern alumnus usually bears the
marks of a good education: the critical mind, the
discerning spirit, a sense of commitment, dedication,
and service. He discusses issues which should be of
concern to the modern alumnus: the quality of life in
America, civil rights and equal opportunity, and
America and the world.

450. "Report of the Fifth General Conference of the
International Atomic Energy Agency, September 26 to
October 6, 1961, Vienna, Austria." 30 pp. Photocopy.
UNDA: CPHS-IAEA.

451. "The Divine Romance of Catholic Education."
Baccalaureate Address . . . Saint Mary's College, 1962.
Notre Dame, Ind.: St. Mary's College, 1962. 7 pp.
Photocopy. UNDA.

452. "Report of the Sixth General Conference of the
International Atomic Energy Agency, September 18 to

September 26, 1962, Vienna, Austria." 23 pp.
Photocopy. UNDA: CPHS-IAEA.

453. "Closing Statement." United States Commission on
      Civil Rights, Washington, D.C., Indianapolis
      Hearings, 29-30 March 1963. 3 pp. Photocopy.
      UNDA.

      Valentine no. 5088.

454. "Gettysburg--Yesterday and Today." Address
      delivered . . . at Gettysburg, Pennsylvania, 29 June
      1963. Carbon. UNDA: UDIS-Biographical Files.

      Delivered at the blessing of a new plaque for the
      statue of Rev. William Corby, C.S.C., past president
      of Notre Dame, who granted eternal absolution to the
      Irish Brigade on 2 July 1863.

455. "My Dear Notre Dame Students." Letter dated 8 April
      1963. Mimeo. UNDA: UDIS-Biographical Files.

      Reviews the local "winter of discontent," responding
      to the spate of troublesome articles appearing in
      Scholastic, a campus publication. Cover letter dated
      8 April 1963 addressed to parent or guardian.

456. "The Theology of Catholic Education." Commencement
      Address delivered . . . at Rosary College Commencement,
      River Forest, Illinois, Friday, 31 May 1963. 15 pp.
      Photocopy. UDIS.

      Catholic education embraces the totality of creation,
      both spirit and matter.

457. "Vocations Interview for Our Sunday Visitor." 1963.
      Carbon. UNDA: UDIS-Biographical Files.

Interview by James Murphy for *Our Sunday Visitor.*

458. "Address given . . . at the Illinois Rally for Civil
Rights, Soldier Field, Sunday, June 21, 1964."
Photocopy. UNDA: UDIS-Biographical Files.

Hesburgh emphasizes the need for dedication to the
dignity of man.

459. "Our Stake in America." Address given . . . at
Commencement Exercises, the University of Wyoming,
1 June 1964. Carbon. UNDA: UDIS-Biographical Files.

Self-respect and a passion for justice are among the
values university graduates should possess.

460. "Report of the Eighth General Conference of the
International Atomic Energy Agency, September 14 to
September 18, 1964, Vienna, Austria." 11 pp.
Photocopy. UNDA: CPHS-IAEA.

461. "Report of the United Nations Third International
Conference on the Peaceful Uses of Atomic Energy,
Geneva, Switzerland, August 31-September 9, 1964."
6 pp. Photocopy. UNDA: CPHS-IAEA.

462. "Address given . . . at Baccalaureate ceremonies,
Indiana University, Sunday, June 13, 1965."
Photocopy. UNDA: UDIS-Biographical Files.

Describes our revolutionary age and its challenges.
Advocates commitment, compassion, and consecration.

463. "Address given . . . at the Commencement Exercises,
Gonzaga University, Spokane, Washington, May 23,
1965." 18 pp. Photocopy. UDIS.

Mature, fully educated Christians must manifest
dedication, involvement, compassion, and concern.

464. "Address . . . on the occasion of Temple University's 79th Commencement . . . Thursday, June 17, 1965, in Philadelphia's Convention Hall . . . ." Philadelphia: Conwellana-Templana Collection, Temple University, 1965. Photocopy. UNDA.

Human equality constitutes the central challenge for our nation today.

465. "Report of the Ninth General Conference of the International Atomic Energy Agency, September 21 to 28, 1965, Tokyo, Japan." 14 pp. Photocopy. UNDA: CPHS-IAEA.

466. "Report of the President, Reverend Theodore M. Hesburgh, C.S.C., at the Tokyo Congress of the International Federation of Catholic Universities, Sophia University, Tokyo, Japan, August 27, 1965." 16 pp. Photocopy. UNDA: CPHS-IFCU.

Hesburgh relects on the organization's past, present, and future.

467. "Sermon delivered at St. Mary's Cathedral, Tokyo, on the occasion of the Mass for Delegates to the Ninth General Conference of the International Atomic Energy Agency, September 26, 1965." 6 pp. Photocopy. UNDA: CPHS-IAEA.

468. "Statement . . . Before the Subcommittee on Science, Research, and Development, House Committee on Science and Astronautics, July 21, 1965." Photocopy. UNDA: UDIS-Biographical Files.

Reviews the accomplishments of the National Science Foundation during its first fifteen years.

469. "Testimony . . . Before Subcommittee No. 5, House Judiciary Committee on H.R. 6400 and Related Bills, Friday, March 19, 1965." 10 pp. Photocopy. UNDA.

Valentine no. 6919.

470. "Personal Statement. Rev. Theodore M. Hesburgh,
C.S.C., Commissioner, U.S. Commission on Civil
Rights." 6 pp. 1966. Photocopy. UNDA.

Hesburgh advocates better education for all with
equal opportunity for all.

Valentine no. 6939.

471. "Report of the Tenth General Conference of the
International Atomic Energy Agency, September 21 to
29, 1966, Vienna, Austria." 10 pp. Photocopy.
UNDA: CPHS-IAEA.

472. "Statement . . . Before the Subcommittee on Departments
of State, Justice, and Commerce, The Judiciary and
Related Agencies Appropriations of the Committee on
Appropriations, U.S. House of Representatives."
12 pp. 1966. Photocopy. UNDA.

Valentine no. 6927.

473. "Dear Members of the Notre Dame Family." Letter dated
18 January 1967. 19 pp. 1967. UNDA: UDIS-Biographical Files.

At an important historical juncture in the history of
the university, when governance passed from clerical
to lay control, Hesburgh discusses the reorganization
of the Board of Trustees. He defines the meaning of
a Catholic university, and the means of achieving its
mission.

474. "Remarks of Reverend Theodore M. Hesburgh, U.S.
Commission on Civil Rights before the National
Conference: Equal Educational Opportunity in
America's Cities, November 16, 1967." 7 pp.
Photocopy. UNDA.

Valentine no. 6950.

475. "Report of the Eleventh General Conference of the
      International Atomic Energy Agency, September 26 to
      October 2, 1967, Vienna, Austria." 18 pp.
      Photocopy. UNDA: CPHS-IAEA.

476. "Dear Notre Dame Faculty Members and Students."
      Letter dated 25 November 1968. UNDA: UDIS-
      Biographical Files.

      Hesburgh confronts the protest against recruiters from
      DOW and CIA. He invites the University community to
      declare itself. "A small minority may exercise
      leadership, but there is a great difference between
      leadership and tyranny. Last Wednesday's performance
      was clearly tyranny."

477. "In Defense of the Younger Generation."
      Remarks . . . Fall Term Commencement, Michigan State
      University, East Lansing, 7 December 1968. East
      Lansing: University Archives and Historical
      Collections, 1968. Photocopy. UNDA.

478. "Report of the Twelfth General Conference of the
      International Atomic Energy Agency, September 24 to
      October 1, 1968, Vienna, Austria." 13 pp. 1968.
      Photocopy. UNDA: CPHS-IAEA.

479. "Statement . . . on the Poor Peoples' March on Washington
      in response to a request from Notre Dame's Student
      Government." 3 pp. 1968. Photocopy. UDIS.

      Hesburgh decries the plight of the blacks, a
      condition which should plague both the individual and
      the collective conscience of Americans.

480. "Address given . . . at the 125th Anniversary Celebration
      of Saint Mary's College, Notre Dame, Indiana,
      December 7, 1969." Photocopy. UNDA.

Hesburgh vividly recalls the history of the early days of St. Mary's and Notre Dame.

481. "Report on the Thirteenth General Conference of the International Atomic Energy Agency, September 23 to September 29, 1969, Vienna, Austria." 10 pp. Photocopy. UNDA: CPHS-IAEA.

482. "Statement . . . Before the Subcommittee on Departments of Labor and Health, Education, and Welfare of the Senate Committee on Appropriations, December 3, 1969." 10 pp. Photocopy. UNDA.

Refers to sections 408 and 409 of H.R. 13111. "The Whitten Amendment would prevent the use of Federal funds by local school districts to implement effective desegregation plans. As such it is harmful and also offends equal protection of the laws under the Constitution of the United States. It should be removed from H.R. 13111 by this Subcommittee." --p. 10.

Valentine no. 6977.

483. "The Words of Chairman Hesburgh." 10 pp. 1969. Photocopy. UNDA.

"This document is based on the transcript of the meeting of the U.S. Commission on Civil Rights held in Phipps House, the University of Denver, Denver, Colorado, June 13-15, 1969."

Valentine no. 6472.

1970-1979

484. "Address given . . . at the Commencement Exercises, Anderson College, Anderson, Indiana, June 15, 1970." 12 pp. Photocopy. UDIS.

Hesburgh centers on love, active in deed and in truth, in the context of Anderson's Tri-S program and Notre Dame's CILA program in Latin America.

485. "Address to the University of Notre Dame faculty . . . on October 5, 1970." UNDA: UDIS-Biographical Files.

Hesburgh calls for greater dedication to teaching in the midst of student and faculty unrest.

486. "Protestants and Catholics Together in Higher Education." 3 pp. 1970? Photocopy. UDIS.

Observes the compatibility of private and public universities and colleges, particularly in Indiana.

487. "Remarks . . . at a student-sponsored rally held May 4, 1970, to discuss U.S. actions in Cambodia." 6 pp. Photocopy. UNDA.

Includes "Declaration" stating six points which support Hesburgh's plea to withdraw military operations in Vietnam, Cambodia, and Laos.

Valentine no. 7004.

488. "Address given . . . at the Annual Convention of the National Foundation of Priests' Councils, Baltimore, Maryland, March 15, 1971." 20 pp. 1971. Photocopy. UDIS.

The suffering in the Church stems not from a crisis of authority or a crisis of leadership, but from a crisis of vision.

489. "Beyond Civil Rights." 10 pp. 1971. Photocopy.

Remarks made before the American Jewish Committee on 13 May 1971.

Valentine no. 6564.

490. [On the Death of Whitney Young.] 2 pp. 1971. Press release. Photocopy. UNDA.

"Whitney Young led the National Urban League during a momentous decade of this country's history. His leadership was a dominant factor in helping our nation come to grips with its racial problems and in assisting black Americans in securing their rightful recognition in the world."--p. 1.

Valentine no. 5274.

491. "Social Responsibility and Continuing Education." Address given . . . at the Conference on Continuing Education at the University of Notre Dame, Notre Dame, Indiana, 8 January 1971. Photocopy. UNDA.

The substance of continuing education for social responsibility requires a moral base: the innate dignity of the human person.

492. Statement . . . on H.R. 9688, the "Housing and Urban Development Act of 1971" before the Housing Subcommittee of the House Banking and Currency Committee, 16 September 1971. 29 pp. Photocopy. UNDA.

Valentine no. 7044.

493. "Statement . . . on S. 2515, the 'Equal Employment Opportunities Enforcement Act of 1971' before the Senate Subcommittee on Labor, October 6, 1971." 9 pp. Photocopy. UNDA.

Valentine no. 7046.

494. "Address . . . Aquinas Assembly, March 7, 1972. Prepared by The Oral History Division, D. Leonard Corgan

Library, King's College, Wilkes-Barre, Pennsylvania."
Wilkes-Barre, Pa.: King's College Library, 1972.
Photocopy. UNDA.

Religious faith and service to others leads to wisdom
and a meaningful life.

495. "America's Unfinished Human Agenda." 25 pp. 1972.
Photocopy. UNDA.

Discusses at length crucial issues in civil rights:
education, busing, housing, unemployment, poverty.
". . . there is no segment of American society where
prejudice and white superiority have ruled more
completely than in housing."--p. 12.

Valentine no. 6666.

496. Statement . . . issued on 21 April in response to
requests from student organizers of anti-Vietnam war
escalation activities on campus. Press release 1 p.
1972. Photocopy. UDIS.

"How long must all this insanity continue? We in
America have lost heavily in lives, resources, and in
the moral rot that has infected our country from
Indo-China actions."

497. Statement . . . New York Hearing, February 1972. 2 pp.
Photocopy. UNDA.

". . . Puerto Rican citizens have suffered too long and
too severely to be deprived of any efforts the
Commission can expend on their behalf."

Valentine no. 7062.

498. "Statement of the United States Commission on Civil
Rights concerning the President's Message to Congress
and Proposed Legislation on Busing and Equal

Educational Opportunities." 17 pp. 1972. Photocopy.
UNDA: UDIS-Biographical Files.

"What has divided the nation on school busing is not
so much sharp disagreement on the merits, but
confusion as to what the issues really are."--p. 1.

499. "Statement . . . on Proposition 21." 3 pp. 1972.
Photocopy. UNDA.

"It is with dismay that I note that Californians are
being asked to vote November 7 on Proposition 21, the
so-called Student School Assignment Initiative."--p. 1.

Valentine no. 7102.

500. "Testimony of Theodore M. Hesburgh, Chairman, U.S.
Commission on Civil Rights, Before the Subcommittee
No. 5 of the House Committee on Judiciary, H.J. Res.
620, March 1, 1972." 18 pp. Photocopy. UNDA.

Hesburgh opposes adoption of proposed amendment
which would relegate "millions of minority school
children into shamefully inferior educational systems
which, only recently, our country had been abandoning
as part of its significant past."--p. 18.

Valentine no. 6656.

501. "A Conference-Call Conversation with Fr. Hesburgh . . .
Wednesday, October 31, 1973." 28 pp. 1973. Photocopy.
UDIS.

Discusses dissent in academia and nonviolence with
several participants from various universities and
colleges in the state of Washington.

502. "Statement . . . before the Subcommittee on International
Organizations and Movements, Foreign Affairs
Committee, United States House of Representatives,

October 11, 1973." 16 pp. Photocopy. UNDA: CPHS-IWO.

Discusses various proposals to strengthen the United
Nations in human rights, and the priority given to
human rights in U.S. foreign policy decision-making.

503. "Address given . . . at the National Catholic Educational
       Association luncheon, St. Louis, Missouri, January
       13, 1974." 6 pp. Photocopy.

       A farewell tribute to Father Clarence William
       Friedman, formerly Vice-President for Higher
       Education of the National Catholic Educational
       Association. UDIS.

504. "Eulogy of James E. Armstrong, '25." January 19,
       1974. 3 pp. Photocopy. UDIS.

       Hesburgh pays final tribute to James E. Armstrong,
       Notre Dame alumnus, chronicler, and secretary of
       the Alumni Association for more than forty-two years,
       noting his fidelity, his humor, and his vision.

505. "Commencement, 1975." Address given at the University
       of Portland, Portland, Oregon, 4 May 1975. Portland:
       University of Portland, 1975. Photocopy. UNDA.

       Examines in depth the value and the fruits of a
       liberal education.

506. "Firing Line." Columbia, S.C.: Southern Educational
       Communications Assoc., 1975. 16 pp. UDIS.

       William F. Buckley, Jr. hosts "Firing Line," with
       Hesburgh as guest, discussing "Food and the Christian
       Conscience." This is a transcript of the "Firing
       Line" program taped in Washington, D.C. on 12 December
       1974 and telecast on PBS on 5 January 1975.

507. "Hall of Fame Banquet, New York City, December 9,
     1975." Address. 7 pp. Photocopy. UDIS.

     Hesburgh reflects on his own early football career
     with his neighborhood team, the Robineau Terriers.
     He shares five principles which he inherited in the
     conduct of intercollegiate athletics.

508. "Sermon delivered . . . at the 'Respect Life' Mass,
     January 22, 1975, in Sacred Heart Church, Notre Dame,
     Indiana." 10 pp. Photocopy. UDIS.

     On the sanctity of human life and the problems of
     abortion.

509. "Statement . . . Before the Subcommittee on Civil and
     Constitutional Rights, House Committee on the
     Judiciary, March 6, 1975." 13 pp. Photocopy. UDIS.

510. "Address given . . . at the Austro-American Committee
     Bicentennial Celebration, Klesheim Palace, Salzburg,
     Austria, July 5, 1976." 22 pp. Photocopy. UDIS.

     Traces the political history of the United States.

511. "Justice in America--the Ideal and the Reality."
     Address given . . . at Denver Summer Commencement,
     13 August 1976. Denver: University of Denver
     Archives, 1976. Photocopy. UNDA.

     ". . . freedom and justice are not dead ashes to be
     revered, but a living flame to be fed by our
     continual dedication and effort."--p. 14.

512. "The University and Society." Convocation Address,
     Laval University, 8 December 1977. 13 pp. Photocopy.
     UDIS.

     Hesburgh explores the principal challenge of change
     facing universities in the midst of contemporary

realities. He expresses hope that universities
will look to philosophical and theological concerns
which ultimately humanize all other concerns.

513. "Address given . . . at St. Francis Xavier University,
      Antigonish, Nova Scotia, Sunday, October 8, 1978."
      Antigonish, N.S.: St. Francis Xavier University
      Archives, 1978. Photocopy. UNDA.

      Describes the conditions of the poorest of the poor
      in the Fourth World, mainly in the Southern
      Hemisphere, and the need to create a better world by
      the next millennium.

514. "Ahuillé. September 18, 1978." 7 pp. 1978. Photocopy.
      UDIS.

      Transcript of translation of Hesburgh's talk at
      Ahuillé. A plaque placed in the baptistry of the church
      of Ahuillé commemorates Rev. Edward F. Sorin, C.S.C.,
      founder of the University of Notre Dame, at his birth-
      place.

515. "The Catholic University in the Modern Context."
      Address given at Duquesne University's Centennial
      Celebration, Pittsburgh, Pennsylvania, 3 October
      1978. Pittsburgh: Duquesne University, 1978.
      Photocopy. UNDA.

      Without a deep respect for philosophy and theology,
      "wholeness of vision will not be ultimately possible,
      nor will a profound sense of human dignity and
      sanctity and integrity prevail."--p. 8.

516. "Homily delivered . . . at the Catholic University of
      Leuven, Leuven, Belgium, on Candlemas Day, February
      2, 1978." 6 pp. Photocopy. UDIS.

      Discusses the liturgical theme of light. "The light
      of the Catholic University in our times must be cast

as broadly as the expansive empire of darkness, and
with no less intelligence than that which espouses
error and promotes evil."--p. 4.

517. "Luncheon Address to Seminar on Multinational
      Managers and Poverty in the Third World, November 3,
      1978." 15 pp. Photocopy. UDIS.

      Discusses the role of multinationals in providing the
      means to create a better world, eliminating widespread
      poverty. Alludes to the Ditchley Foundation Lectures
      on Interdependence (Oxfordshire, England, September
      1974) which lay out a set of conditions "under which
      multinationals could be considered prime engines of
      development."--p. 8.

518. "Statement of Theodore M. Hesburgh, C.S.C. . . . Chairman
      of the Overseas Development Council before the Senate
      Foreign Relations Committee on the International
      Development Cooperation Act of 1978--S. 2420."
      49 pp. Photocopy. UNDA: CPHS-ODC.

519. "Statement of Theodore M. Hesburgh, of Indiana, for
      the Rank of Ambassador During the Tenure of His
      Service as Chairman of the United States Delegation
      to United Nations Conference on Science and
      Technology." 9 pp. 1978. Photocopy. UDIS.

      Hesburgh responds to questions from Senators Stone,
      Percy, Case, and others regarding the forthcoming U.N.
      Conference on Science and Technology for Development.

520. "Address by Ambassador Theodore M. Hesburgh, Chairman,
      U.S. Delegation to the United Nations Conference on
      Science and Technology for Development, Vienna,
      August 20, 1979." 8 pp. Photocopy. UDIS.

      "The task of this conference is not one of restating
      the errors of the past but of weaving science and
      technology into the fabric of the future, the fabric

of development. We need collaboration, not confrontation."--p. 4.

521. "Address given . . . at the National Conference on Church Related Colleges and Universities, Notre Dame, Indiana, June 21, 1979." 11 pp. Photocopy. UDIS.

522. "Address given . . . at the 75th Anniversary of Assumption College, Worcester, Massachusetts, September 18, 1979." Worcester: Assumption College Library, 1979. Photocopy. UNDA.

Traces the evolution of Catholic universities throughout the world. Probes the question: "What does it mean to be a Catholic university?"

523. "Address given . . . on the occasion of receiving the College Board Medal for Distinguished Service to Education, New Orleans, Louisiana, October 29, 1979." 5 pp. Photocopy. UDIS.

On quality, equality, and Affirmative Action.

524. Letter to The Honorable Jimmy Carter, President of the United States, dated January 9, 1979. 3 pp. Photocopy. UDIS.

As chairman of the Board, Overseas Development Council, Hesburgh states his concern regarding two major challenges the United States faces with developing countries for which no clear U.S. policy is apparent. Carter's reply of 23 January 1979 is appended.

525. "Proposed Institute for Technological Cooperation." 4 pp. 1979? Photocopy. UDIS.

"The goal will be not only to help developing countries to use science and technology more effectively, but also to mobilize a larger share of America's scientific and technological strength to

assist in the alleviation of global poverty, and in
support of development."--p. 1.

526.   "Remarks made . . . at the Ecumenical Service following
the Signing of the Peace Treaty, Lincoln Memorial,
Washington, D.C., March 26, 1979." 4 pp. Photocopy.
UDIS.

Throughout the world, religious persons must be
profoundly committed to one simple reality: peace.

527.   "Testimony on the Institute for Technological
Cooperation, Senate Foreign Relations Committee,
March 15, 1979." 7 pp. Photocopy. UDIS.

Favors the IFTC proposal which "represents a U.S.
intiative toward putting science and technology to
work more effectively on development problems and
that is at the heart of the purpose of UNCSTD."--
p. 5.

1980-1988

528.   "Address given . . . at the Commemoration Day exercises,
marking the 104th Anniversary of the founding of The
Johns Hopkins University, February 22, 1980." 12 pp.
Photocopy. UNDA. UDIS.

Cites government aid of more than $200 million to
Cambodia as an example of voluntary leadership between
public and private, national and international organizations.

For audio, see item no. 401.

529.   "Address given . . . at the 63rd Annual Founder's Day
Service, Tuskegee Institute, Tuskegee Institute,
Alabama, March 30, 1980." 8 pp. Photocopy. UDIS.

"Luther Foster and I shared another dream . . . namely that human dignity and human rights and human hope could be a reality for all black Americans."--p. 2.

530. "Address given . . . on the occasion of the United States Military Academy 1980 Thayer Award, West Point, New York, September 11, 1980." 7 pp. Photocopy. UDIS.

"Make no mistake about it, true patriotism, especially in the military, requires great inner spiritual strength and enlightened leadership."--p. 5.

531. "Address given . . . on the occasion of the United Way of America Alexis de Tocqueville Award, Toronto, Canada, April 21, 1980." 14 pp. Photocopy. UDIS.

On voluntarism.

532. "The Catholic University in the Modern Context." Commencement Address, University of San Diego, 25 May 1980. San Diego: University of San Diego, 1980. Photocopy. UNDA.

533. "When an Entire People Dies . . . . There Can Be No Excuses." 4 pp. 1980? Photocopy. UDIS.

As cochairman, National Cambodian Crisis Committee, Hesburgh vividly describes the devastation in Cambodia and outlines two excellent opportunities for nations, institutions, and individuals to take constructive action in preventing the loss of an entire race of people.

534. "Address given . . . at the Annual Convention of the National Association of Secondary School Principals, Atlanta, Georgia, February 23, 1981." Photocopy. UDIS.

Discusses quality and equality as the most important challenge facing American education on all levels.

For video, see item no. 404. For audio, see item no.
405.

535. "Address given . . . at the Summer Commencement,
University of Michigan, Ann Arbor, Michigan, August
23, 1981." 12 pp. Photocopy. UDIS.

Hesburgh reviews four fundamental questions of
concern to the U.S. Commission on Immigration and
Refugee Policy: "1) How many immigrants and refugees
should be admitted to the United States annually; 2)
From where; 3) By what procedures; and 4) What should
be the criteria governing the answers to the first
three questions?"--p. 4.

536. "Commencement Address. University of Scranton,
Pennsylvania." Scranton, Pa.: University Archives,
1981. 6 pp. Photocopy. [Press release.]

Hesburgh stresses the value of love, competence,
compassion, and commitment.

537. "Discurso do Padre Theodore Martin Hesburgh."
Universidade de Brasília, Campus Universitário, Asa
Norte, 70910 Brasília. 4 pp. 1981. Photocopy. UNDA.

Hesburgh eulogizes academia as a source of learning and
wisdom. Address delivered at solemn session of the
University Council on 15 December 1981.

538. "The Future of the Liberal Arts Education." Address
given at Seattle University, Seattle, Washington,
23 April 1981. Seattle: Seattle University, 1981.
Photocopy. 14 pp. UNDA.

Hesburgh discusses the nature of liberal education,
describing its characteristics, its fruits, and its
inherent sense of values. "Liberation from life's
frustrations, and the special crosses that attend
every individual life, is no small part of the total

liberation that can result from a liberal education
--to be really human."--p. 10.

539. "Homily delivered . . . at the Funeral Mass for Bernard
J. Voll, Sacred Heart Church, Notre Dame, Indiana,
September 23, 1981." UDIS.

"He was the oldest and most beloved of the Trustees
of this University--two years short of forty years
of service as regular and emeritus Trustee and
Fellow, Vice Chairman of the Board, and Chairman of
the Investment Committee for twenty years."--p. 2.

540. "Voluntarism: An American Legacy." Address given . . . on
the Chicago Sunday Evening Club television program,
6 December 1981. Taped 22 November 1981. 9 pp.
Photocopy. UDIS.

"There is an integral, organic unity to the life of a
Christian. In the broadest sense, the committed
Christian is, like Christ the Savior, engaged in the
creation of a new world and new man."--p. 8.

541. "Your Excellency." Cover letter dated 24 July 1981.
Document dated 4 July 1981. 25 pp. Photocopy. UDIS.

Memorandum addressed to all members of the Catholic
hierarchy concerning the unfolding of a policy for
Catholic higher education. "This essay is an attempt
to put into historical perspective the distant and
recent past of Catholic universities in the world,
the present status of these universities, particularly as developed during the decade following 1963, and
the new proposed canons of Canon Law as they affect
this present status."--p. 1.

542. "Address given . . . at the Inauguration of Father Thomas
Oddo, C.S.C., President, University of Portland,
Portland, Oregon, October 10, 1982." Portland:
University of Portland, 1982. Photocopy. UNDA.

Reviews the qualities of leadership essential for the presidency of a university.

543. "Address given . . . at the 25th Anniversary Commemorative Meeting of the Pugwash Movement, Pugwash, Nova Scotia, on July 16, 1982." Typescript. UDIS.

Upon hearing of the medical effects of a one megaton bomb explosion, Hesburgh's commitment to work unceasingly toward the elimination of the nuclear threat became his highest priority.

544. "The Catholic Church and Education." Address given . . . at the National Catholic Educational Association Convention, Chicago, Illinois, 14 April 1982. 13 pp. Photocopy. UDIS.

Surveys the past and future challenges of Catholic education.

545. "Religion and Science Against Nuclear Weapons," by Theodore M. Hesburgh and Victor Weisskopf. 3 pp. 1982. Photocopy. UDIS.

546. "Will Liberal Arts Survive?" Speech presented at Loretto Heights College Heights Week '82 Banquet, October 13, 1982, Denver, Colorado. Denver: Loretto Heights College, 1982. Photocopy. UNDA.

Stresses the need for critical thinking, the importance of the study of philosophy and theology, and the ability to situate oneself.

547. "Colgate University, Baccalaureate Address, May 29, 1983." Hamilton, N.Y.: Case Library, Colgate University, 1983. Photocopy. UNDA.

To serve others well is the only way we can really love God. Hesburgh advises graduates to remember simply three things: "to be competent, to be compassionate, and to be committed . . . ."--p. 7.

548. "Homily preached . . . at the Dedication Mass for the
      Notre Dame London Law Centre July 29, 1983." 5 pp.
      Photocopy. UDIS.

      A truly professional person is compassionate,
      suffering with those who suffer, and open to those
      who need help.

549. "The Moral Dimensions of Higher Education." Address
      given at the first meeting of the Association of
      Universities and Colleges of Canada and the American
      Council on Education, Toronto, 13 October 1983.
      Photocopy. UDIS.

550. "Testimony of The Reverend Theodore M. Hesburgh,
      C.S.C., Co-Chairman of the Citizens' Committee for
      Immigration Reform, Before the Senate Subcommittee on
      Immigration and Refugee Policy, Washington, D.C.,
      February 25, 1983." Photocopy. UDIS.

      Hesburgh agrees that refugee admissions should not
      be dependent on any fixed ceiling on numbers of legal
      immigrants. Summarizes eight positive aspects of
      legal immigration.

551. "Commencement Address Delivered April 28, 1984."
      Saint Leo College, Saint Leo, Florida. Saint Leo,
      Fla.: Saint Leo College, 1984. Photocopy. UNDA.

      Cites examples of poverty throughout the world. The
      essence of a meaningful life is a life of competence,
      compassion, and consecration.

552. "Rev. Theodore M. Hesburgh's Speech, Law Day, May 1,
      1984. Business and Professional People for the Public
      Interest, Chicago, Illinois." Photocopy. UDIS.

Hesburgh graphically describes the reality of the
nuclear threat. "Simply put, we are threatened with
extinction."

553. "Address delivered . . . at the Commencement Exercises,
Duke University, Durham, North Carolina, May 5,
1985." 12 pp. Photocopy. UNDA.

Hesburgh vividly describes the plight of the blacks
during the fifties and sixties and the cause for
civil rights.

554. "Address delivered . . . at the 40th Anniversary dinner
of *The Bulletin of the Atomic Scientists*, Chicago,
Illinois, December 12, 1985." Photocopy. UDIS.

Well-documented address on the history of the nuclear
dilemma. In 1985, Hesburgh founded the Institute for
International Peace Studies, University of Notre
Dame, which actively continues the dialogue between
scientific and religious leaders.

555. "Address delivered . . . at the 70th Annual Conference of
the National University Continuing Education
Association, Louisville, Kentucky, April 16, 1985."
Photocopy. UDIS.

Summarizes report of the Carnegie Commission on the
Future of Higher Education, published in 1973,
entitled "The Progress and the Performance of Higher
Education in the United States: Approaching the Year
2000."

556. "Corporate and Campus Cooperation: The Challenge
Ahead." An Address by Rev. Theodore M. Hesburgh,
C.S.C. . . . . Chairman, Business-Higher Education Forum.
American Council on Education 86th Annual Meeting,
28 October 1985, Miami Beach, Florida. Photocopy.
UDIS.

The existence of the Business-Higher Education Forum symbolizes the importance of continuing contact between corporations and educational institutions in cooperative ventures.

557. "Eugene Burke Lecture Series: Inaugural Lecture." University of San Diego, 3 April 1985. Photocopy. UDIS.

Address on the nuclear threat to humanity and the moral dimension of higher education.

558. "Peace Corps--ROTC Style." Address given at a Peace Corps observance in Washington D.C., 21 September 1986. Photocopy. UDIS.

"I believe the time has come to institutionalize the Peace Corps and set it firmly into American life, as surely as the Post Office exists as a permanent reality . . . I take as my model the ROTC Program . . . ."--p. 2.

559. "Address given . . . at the Spring Annual Conference of the Association of Governing Boards of Universities and Colleges, New Orleans, March 22, 1987." 12 pp. Photocopy. UDIS.

Surveys the history and function of Notre Dame's Board of Trustees which has been under lay governance since 1967.

560. "In the Heart of the City." Address . . . at the 200th Commencement of the University of Pittsburgh, Pittsburgh, Pennsylvania, 10 May 1987. 12 pp. Photocopy. UDIS.

Considers the role of the urban university in dealing with poverty, illiteracy, and other sociological problems sweeping the nation.

For audio, see item no. 426.

561. "Remarks to the Heisman Memorial Trophy Award Dinner
--December 10, 1987, New York Marriott Marquis
Hotel." 7 pp. Photocopy. UDIS.

Notre Dame boasts seven Heisman Trophy winners with
Tim Brown's award in 1987. Hesburgh comments on
Rev. Edmund Joyce's proposal to monitor collegiate
athletics.

562. "Valedictory to Alumni and Friends . . . During a
Satellite Television Broadcast from Washington Hall
May 9, 1987." Photocopy. UNDA.

In taking leave of his office as president of the
University of Notre Dame, Hesburgh envisions the task
of today and tomorrow as one directed "to deepen, to
intensify, to broaden our human understanding of the
treasure of faith."

For video, see item no. 429.

563. "Address given . . . for the Morgenthau Memorial
Lecture, Carnegie Council on Ethics and International
Affairs, New York City, Novermer 3, 1988." 25 pp.
UNDA

Hesburgh discusses at length the history and evolution of the nuclear dilemma since its inception in
1945.

Diaries by Theodore M. Hesburgh

1970-1979

564. Diary of Theodore M. Hesburgh, 19 July 1973-
11 August 1973. St. Lucia (Caribbean), Salvador,
N.E. Brazil, Senegal, Mauritania, and Mali.
Notre Dame, Ind.: Department of Public Relations and
Information, University of Notre Dame, 1973. 73 pp.
Photocopy.

565. Diary of Theodore M. Hesburgh, 8 July 1978-16 August
1978. "Trip to South Africa, July 8-22, 1978.
Sponsored by the U.S.-South African Leader Exchange
Program." Notre Dame, Ind.: Office of the President,
University of Notre Dame, 1978. 167 pp. Photocopy.

566. Diary of Theodore M. Hesburgh, 21 June 1979-
11 July 1979. Mainland China. Notre Dame, Ind.:
Department of Public Relations and Information,
University of Notre Dame, 1979. 123 pp. Photocopy.

1980-1989

567. Diary of Theodore M. Hesburgh, 1 July 1980-1 August
1980. Alaska, Hawaii, Guam, Manila, Kampuchea
(Cambodia), Bangkok, Thailand, and Singapore. Notre
Dame, Ind.: Department of Public Relations and

Information, University of Notre Dame, 1980.
Photocopy. 188 pp. UNDA.

"My hat as Chairman of the U.S. Select Committee on
Immigration and Refugee Policy was mainly worn in
America Samoa, Guam, and Saipan. My Rockefeller
Foundation Chairman hat was worn in Bangkok." --
Cover letter.

568. Diary of Theodore M. Hesburgh, 25 March 1982-30 March
1982. "The San Salvador Elections: A Diary." Notre
Dame, Ind.: Department of Public Relations and
Information, University of Notre Dame, 1982. 29 pp.
Photocopy. UNDA.

569. Diary of Theodore M. Hesburgh, 15 July 1982-31 August
1982. Aboard the *Esso Picardi* from Genoa to Ras
Tanura, Saudi Arabia. With Father Pat Gaffney to
Yemen, Oman, Abu Dhabi, Dubai, Bahrain, Jordan, and
Vienna. Notre Dame, Ind.: Department of Public
Relations and Information, University of Notre Dame,
1982. 122 pp. Photocopy. UNDA.

570. Diary of Father Hesburgh's trip to China, Nepal,
India, the Seychelles, and Kenya, 26 June-23 July
1984. Notre Dame, Ind.: Department of Public
Relations and Information, University of Notre Dame,
1984. 125 pp. Photocopy. UNDA.

571. Diary of Theodore M. Hesburgh. Trip to Moscow
and Beijing 2 July 1986-21 July 1986. Notre Dame,
Ind.: Department of Public Relations and Information,
University of Notre Dame, 1986. 85 pp. Photocopy.

"The two main foci of the trip were Moscow and
Beijing where we were engaged in enlisting the
cooperation of the Russian and the Chinese Academies
of Sciences to support our work in Notre Dame's new
Institute for International Peace Studies."--Cover
letter dated 5 September 1986.

572.   "Travels With Ted and Ned, I. North America." Notre
       Dame, Ind: Department of Public Relations and
       Information, University of Notre Dame, 1987. 197 pp.
       Photocopy.

       Hesburgh's diary dated 11 June 1987 through 31 August
       1987 records his journey with Rev. Edmund P. Joyce
       through the Western United States and Alaska.

573.   "Travels with Ted and Ned, II. Central and South
       America." Notre Dame, Ind.: Department of Public
       Relations and Information, University of Notre Dame,
       1988. 198 pp. Photocopy.

       Cover letter dated July 1988. Diary dated 26 September
       1987-5 December 1987 covers the second segment of
       Hesburgh's sabbatical year during which he traveled
       extensively with Rev. Edmund P. Joyce throughout
       Latin America from Mexico to Tierra del Fuego.

574.   "Travels With Ted and Ned, III. The Caribbean at
       Christmas Time." Notre Dame, Ind.: Office of the
       President Emeritus, University of Notre Dame, 1320
       Hesburgh Library, 1988. 36 pp. Photocopy.

       Cover letter dated October 1988. Diary dated 19
       December 1987-7 January 1988 includes Hesburgh's
       account of events during a shakedown cruise through
       the Caribbean on the ocean liner *Queen Elizabeth II*.
       The purpose of this cruise with Rev. Edmund Joyce was
       to become familiar with "this marvelous but very
       complicated ship . . . . the story is mainly our
       becoming acquainted with what we would be doing as
       Chaplains of the QE2."--Cover letter. Includes account
       of their visits to Martinique, Barbados, Cartegena,
       Curaçao, and Amsterdam.

575.   "Travels With Ted and Ned, IV. Around the World on the
       QE2." Notre Dame, Ind.: Office of the President
       Emeritus, University of Notre Dame, 1320 Hesburgh

Library, 1988. 277 pp. Photocopy.

Cover letter dated October 1988. Diary dated 13 January 1988-2 May 1988. As Chaplains of the QE2, Hesburgh and Rev. Edmund Joyce cruise "across the world," visiting various ports, including the South Island of New Zealand; Australia; Mombasa, East Africa; Beijing; Korea; Osaka, Yokohama, and Tokyo, Japan; and Hawaii. "This trip took over a hundred days and involved some 30,000 miles of travel by sea. Needless to say, it was good to get home again where we are now busily working on a wide variety of projects."--Cover letter.

576. Diary of Theodore M. Hesburgh. "Antarctica - December 1988." Notre Dame, Ind.: Office of the President Emeritus, University of Notre Dame, 1320 Hesburgh Library, 1989. 47 pp. Photocopy.

Diary dated 14 December 1988-30 December 1988. Provides an account of Hesburgh's trip with Rev. Edmund Joyce to Antarctica. "As a kind of postscript to the three versions of the diaries you have already received, here is the final version. Ned and I were invited by the Society Explorer group to be the first Chaplains they ever have had on a trip. It's the same little red ship we had on the Amazon and this time the trip was to the Antarctic Peninsula South of Chile."--Cover letter dated February 1989.

Hesburgh's diaries are generally distributed to various individuals affiliated with the University of Notre Dame.

Books About Theodore M. Hesburgh

1970-1979

577. Connelly, Joel, and Howard J. Dooley. *Hesburgh's Notre Dame: Triumph in Transition*. New York: Hawthorn Books, 1972.

   Written by two Notre Dame graduates, this work purports to be "a collection of impressions and vignettes" about Hesburgh during the era of campus revolution.

578. Armstrong, James E. *Onward to Victory: A Chronicle of the Alumni of the University of Notre Dame du Lac, 1842-1973*. Notre Dame, Ind.: University of Notre Dame, 1974.

   In his foreword to this work, Hesburgh states "It is not a history of the University although there is a lot of Notre Dame lore in it. Rather it is a warm and often witty account of the role alumni have played in the development of Notre Dame from an obscure frontier school to an internationally celebrated universitity." --p. ix. Primarily about Hesburgh's milieu, it contains valuable background information and references to works related to the history of Notre Dame.

579.   Notre Dame, Ind. University. Center for Civil Rights.
       *Directory: Theodore M. Hesburgh Civil Rights
       Collection.* Compiled by William R. Valentine. Notre
       Dame, Ind.: Notre Dame Law School, Center for Civil
       Rights, 1976.

       "This collection represents 25 years of personal
       contact with civil and human rights activities,
       including 17 years on the United States Commission on
       Civil Rights. There are approximately 200,000 frames
       of microfilmed pages in the Hesburgh collection,
       representing nearly 14,000 documents."--p. viii.
       Lists reports, publications, press releases,
       statements, clippings, correspondence, proposals,
       pamphlets, and other materials pertinent to
       Hesburgh's membership on the U.S. Civil Rights
       Commission.

580.   Karam, Thomas Joseph. "A Rhetorical Analysis of
       Selected Speeches on Higher Education by Reverend
       Theodore M. Hesburgh." Master's thesis, Department of
       Speech, Louisiana State University and Agricultural
       and Mechanical College, 1979. 82 pp.

                          1980-1988

581.   University of Notre Dame. Library. *Hesburgh
       Bibliography.* Notre Dame, Ind: University of Notre
       Dame, 1980.

       Compiled by Charlotte A. Ames, Wendy Clauson
       Schlereth, and Thomas T. Spencer, this bibliography
       includes selected works by and about Hesburgh from
       about 1940 until June 1980.

582.   Wofford, Harris. *Of Kennedys and Kings: Making Sense
       of the Sixties.* New York: Farrar, Straus, Giroux,
       1980.

Contains numerous references to Hesburgh and his role
in national affairs. The appendix, "Precursor and
Conscience: The Commission on Civil Rights" (pp. 461-
83), provides valuable background information on
Hesburgh's work on the Civil Rights Commission.

583.   Quay, Richard H. *On the American College Presidency:
A Bibliography of Theodore M. Hesburgh.* Public
Administration Series: Bibliography P-1361.
Monticello, Ill.: Vance Bibliographies, 1984.

"This bibliography, although titled for his contributions
to scholarship on the college presidency, also includes
books and essays on civil rights and other social and
economic issues."--p. 1.

584.   Lundquist, M. Suzanne Everston. "The Trickster: A
Transformation Archetype." Ph.D. diss., University of
Michigan, 1985.

Discusses studies by the Carnegie Foundation and the
Rockefeller Foundation which indicate modern Western
man's pressing need to reevaluate his nature.
Hesburgh offers a solution to the problem of human
isolation and fragmentation.

See *Dissertation Abstracts International* 46, sec. A,
p. 983 for abstract.

585.   [A Notre Dame Moment.] Notre Dame, Ind.: Alumni
Association, University of Notre Dame, 1987. 12 pp.
UNDA.

"This booklet was designed to accompany Father
Hesburgh's valedictory to Notre Dame students, alumni
and friends from Washington Hall on the Notre Dame
campus May 9, 1987."

For valedictory address, see item no. 562.

586. Lungren, John C., Jr., *Hesburgh of Notre Dame: Priest, Educator, Public Servant.* Kansas City: Sheed and Ward, 1987.

A biography of Hesburgh which highlights his early life, his presidential years at Notre Dame, student unrest, service on the Civil Rights Commission, the Presidential Clemency Board, the Select Commission on Immigration, social justice, and other aspects of his career.

Articles About Theodore M. Hesburgh

1940-1949

587. "Officers of the Veterans' Club Poised on the Steps of Walsh Hall." *Scholastic* 87 (12 April 1946): 19.

    Photograph of Hesburgh, Chaplain of Veterans' Club, with Jim Webb, president, and other members of the club.

588. "Hesburgh Heads Department of Religion." *Scholastic* 90 (8 October 1948): 11.

    Hesburgh, prominent as a nationally recognized speaker on Catholic Action, replaces Rev. Roland G. Simonitsch as head of the Department of Religion.

1950-1959

589. "The New President: A Study in Confidence." *Scholastic* 94 (26 September 1952): 15, 23.

    Contains biographical information on Hesburgh's early life and career.

590. "Notre Dame Has New President." *Catholic School Journal* 52 (September 1952): 36A.

At age 35, Hesburgh succeeds Rev. John J. Cavanaugh, C.S.C., as president of the University of Notre Dame. Includes photograph.

591. "Fr. Hesburgh Receives Citation." *Scholastic* 95 (7 May 1954): 17.

Hesburgh received the annual Brotherhood Award of the South Bend-Mishawaka Roundtable of the National Conference of Christians and Jews.

592. "Annual Marriage Institute Will Open Feb. 23; Noted Lecturers to Speak at Seven Sessions." *Scholastic* 96 (14 January 1955): 14.

Hesburgh to address the Institute on Courtship and Engagement. His talk is "yearly acclaimed as one of the best."--p. 14.

593. "New Sculpture Studio for Mestrovic." *Scholastic* 97 (30 September 1955): 30.

Hesburgh announces a gift of $75,000 from I. A. O'Shaughnessy, St. Paul, Minn., to house the works of Ivan Mestrovic.

594. "Hustler for Quality." *Time* 67 (7 May 1956): 77-78.

Reviews Hesburgh's efforts to raise academic standards.

595. "Civil Rights: New Instrument." *Time* 70 (18 November 1957): 28.

Hesburgh photographed with Stanley F. Reed, John A. Hanna, John S. Battle, Ernest Wilkins, and Robert Gerald Storey, all members of the bipartisan Civil Rights Commission created by the Civil Rights Act, 17 September 1957.

596. Smith, Dick. "Atoms for Peace." *Scholastic* 99
(15 November 1957): 20-21.

Reports on Hesburgh's participation in the first
General Conference of the International Atomic Energy
Agency as a representative of the Vatican. Includes
photographs of Hesburgh, Pope Pius XII, Frank Folsom,
and others.

597. "Citizens Give Ideas in Crisis." *Life* 44 (13 January
1958): 13-20.

An overview of the seven-part Rockefeller Report on
problems and opportunities confronting America.
Hesburgh calls Report II, on international security,
"a philosophical approach to the whole problem of
power."--p. 14.

598. "Father Hesburgh Renamed as President of the
University." *Scholastic* 99 (2 May 1958): 9.

Rev. Theodore J. Mehling, C.S.C., Provincial Superior
of the Holy Cross Fathers, announces Hesburgh's re-
appointment. Hesburgh's accomplishments and future
goals are summarized.

1960-1969

599. Dyer, F.C. "How Many Were Listening?" *America* 103
(28 May 1960): 301.

Dyer reports on Hesburgh's speech at the Catholic
Press Association's annual luncheon on 11 May in
Washington. Hesburgh discussed modern science, the
U. N. Bill of Rights, U.S. civil rights, and quality
in higher education.

600. "Repeat Performance." *America* 102 (30 January 1960):
517.

Report on Hesburgh's clarification of the moral issues involved in population control.

601. Lomask, Milton. "Theology and Science Intersect at a Point Called Hesburgh." *Sign* 40 (March 1961): 16-18, 72.

Biographical account of Hesburgh's career, with emphasis on his interest in science.

602. "Moral Dimension." *Time* 77 (21 April 1961): 37-38.

Article summarizes Hesburgh's career and his effort to maintain the moral dimension of Catholic teaching. *Time* quotes Hesburgh as saying that "the trouble with U.S. Catholic colleges is an 'abysmal mediocrity' that has made them 'almost universally destitute of intellectual leadership.'"

In a night letter to *Time*, Hesburgh objects that he was quoted out of context with reference to "abysmal mediocrity," which was "part of a long historical summary on the ups and downs of Catholic higher learning, not an indictment of present day efforts." --Night letter, T. M. Hesburgh, C.S.C., to Editor, *Time*. UNDA: UDIS Biographical Files.

603. Thorman, Donald J. "Education for the Space Age." *Voice of St. Jude* 26 (February 1961): 7-14. UNDA: UDIS-Biographical Files.

Discusses Hesburgh's role in civil rights, international relations, and American Catholic higher education.

604. "A Challenge to Science." *America* 107 (1 December 1962): 1166.

Report of Hesburgh's address at the National Science Foundation dinner. Hesburgh asks scientists and engineers "to question the moral impact of their work on the world of man in which they live."

605. "God & Man at Notre Dame." *Time* 79: (9 February 1962): 48-54.

Cover story on Hesburgh's dramatic success in promoting academic excellence at Notre Dame.

606. Kretzmann, O. P. "Student Freedom." *Commonweal* 78 (28 June 1963): 379.

Kretzmann, president of Valparaiso University, refers to *Commonweal* editorial "Student Freedom" (31 May). Kretzmann states emphatically that "the students are wrong--even tragically wrong--and Father Hesburgh is right. Here is the outcropping on a Catholic campus of the heresy of freedom without responsibility."--p. 379.

607. Star, Jack. "Trouble Ahead for the Catholic Schools." *Look* 27 (22 October 1963): 37-40.

Hesburgh stresses the need for first-rate Catholic education.

608. "Student Freedom." *Commonweal* 78 (31 May 1963): 269-70.

Commonweal sympathizes with student protests at Notre Dame, objecting to the suppression of a number of articles in *Scholastic*, Notre Dame's student magazine. "The unfortunate part of the university's response to the students was that it tried to counter their excesses with the traditional formula of suppression and admonition."--p. 270.

609. "This Side of the Vision." *Time* 81 (3 May 1963): 88.

In the midst of student discontent over faculty censorship
of three articles in *Scholastic*, Hesburgh confirms
that the primary role of students is to learn, not to
teach.

610. "Vicious Circles of Father Hesburgh." *Christian
Century* 80 (14 August 1963): 1015.

Cites O. P. Kretzmann's defense of Hesburgh in
Commonweal (28 June 1963). Hesburgh's vicious
circles include student attitudes toward football
and academic excellence, Hesburgh's absenteeism,
and student freedom.

611. "Why Not 'Chancellor' Hesburgh?" *Scholastic* 104
(22 February 1963): 7-8.

Proposes appointment of a renowned lay administrator
of the stature of George N. Shuster, Hesburgh's
administrative assistant, to guide academic
development. Suggests that Hesburgh be named
chancellor.

612. "Itinerary International." *Scholastic* 106 (18 September 1964): 13, 24-25.

Describes Hesburgh's summer itinerary: Geneva, Vienna,
Rome, and Washington. Hesburgh received the
Presidential Medal of Freedom on 14 September 1964.

613. "Memorial March." *Scholastic* 105 (22 May 1964): 14.

As principal speaker at a civil rights demonstration
in downtown South Bend, Hesburgh commended the
Supreme Court decision which prohibited segregation
in public schools.

614. "Notre Dame's Irish Dander Rises Over a Movie." *Life*
57 (18 December 1964): 68, 72a.

Hesburgh seeks an injunction against the distribution of *John Goldfarb, Please Come Home,* a $4 million spoof depicting Notre Dame football players amidst belly dancers and harem girls at Fauz U.

615. "As Seen by His Friends." In *Testimonial Program,* edited by Mel Noel, James Berberet, and Barry Johanson, 6-7. Notre Dame, Ind.: n.p., 1965.

Consists of several tributes offered in honor of Hesburgh at the Student Testimonial Banquet held on 28 April 1965. Tributes by John A. Hannah, President, Michigan State University, and others.

616. Murray, Dan. "Fr. Theodore Hesburgh--the Man." In *Testimonial Program,* edited by Mel Noel, James Berberet, and Barry Johanson, 4-5. Notre Dame, Ind.: n.p., 1965.

617. Noel, Mel. "His Vision for Notre Dame." In *Testimonial Program,* edited by Mel Noel, James Berberet, and Barry Johanson, 10. Notre Dame, Ind.: n.p., 1965.

618. Paul VI, Pope. "To Our Son, Theodore Hesburgh, President of the University of Notre Dame and President of the International Association of Catholic Universities." 6 pp. 1965. UDIS.

Apostolic Blessing imparted 24 August 1965. "The Catholic university should pursue its inquiries in full concert with all the universities of the world . . . . In all of this activity, the university must reach hearts, since wisdom, the university's highest gift, is intelligence enkindled in love."-- pp. 5-6.

619. Twohey, John. "His Worldwide Involvement." In *Testimonial Program,* edited by Mel Noel, James Berberet, and Barry Johanson, 8-9. Notre Dame, Ind.:

n.p., 1965.

620.   Schrag, Peter. "Notre Dame: Our First Great Catholic University?" *Harper's Magazine* 234 (May 1967): 41-49.

621.   Deedy, John. "News and Views." *Commonweal* 89 (20 December 1968): 390.

Deedy comments on Hesburgh's encounter with delgates at the National Student Association conference. "The exchange didn't go well. The students were particularly unsettled by a Hesburgh statement that he could see no connection between Reserve Officer Training Corps classes and racism."

622.   "Fr. Hesburgh's News Conference." *America* 119 (16 November 1968): 464.

623.   Hainline, Forrest. "Thoughts IV." *Scholastic* 109 (5 April 1968): 20-21.

The author quotes extensively from Hesburgh's booklet *Thoughts IV,* which discusses the nature of a Catholic university. He concludes that "Fr. Hesburgh's contradiction-filled essays simply provide further evidence that a Catholic university is indeed a contradiction in terms."--p. 21.

624.   Macaulay, Michael G. and Lloyd A. Wagner. "Clearly Tyranny." *Scholastic* 110 (6 December 1968): 7.

Two graduate students criticize Hesburgh's letter to Notre Dame's faculty and students concerning the Dow-CIA demonstrations.

625.   Campion, D. R. "Of Many Things: Letter to the University Faculty and Student Body." *America* 120 (8 March 1969): Inside cover.

626. Connelly, Joel. "The Fjords of Southern Chile."
      Scholastic 110 (21 March 1969): 13.

      Hesburgh is criticized in his role as newly appointed
      head of the Civil Rights Commission.

627. Connelly, Joel, and Thomas Payne. "The Controlling
      Hand." *Scholastic* 110 (14 February 1969): 16, 24.

      Despite division of authority, Hesburgh "continues to
      exercise supreme control of University affairs."--
      p. 24.

628. Connelly, Joel, Thomas Payne, and William Cullen. "An
      Essay on the Conception and Implementation of
      Community." *Scholastic* 110 (21 March 1969): 18-24, 4.

      The student authors criticize Hesburgh's concept of
      community.

629. "Father Hesburgh's True Position." *America* 120 (15
      March 1969): 291.

      Discusses Hesburgh's letter to Vice-President Agnew
      regarding supression of violence and vandalism on
      college campuses. Hesburgh advised that "local
      and Federal governments act on two assumptions: first,
      that the university community is able to formulate
      its own guidelines for managing student protestors;
      and second, that when special outside help is needed,
      the university will request it quickly and efficently,
      but only as a last alternative to internal self-correction
      . . . . It falsifies Fr. Hesburgh's position to describe
      it as a 'get tough' policy. He is really calling for
      reasonableness and civility."

630. "Hesburgh's Law." *Commonweal* 89 (14 March 1969):
      719-20.

Labels Hesburgh's "policy of threat" delusionary.
"The student witness is minimized and nothing more
enlightened is expected from the administration than
the policies which are the sickness of the nation and
the very causes of really serious campus confrontations: institutional racism, exploitation of science,
collusion with the military, etc."--pp. 719-20.

631.   Moran, Rich. "The Last Word." *Scholastic* 111 (3
October 1969): 30.

Scholastic editor both supports and criticizes
Hesburgh on his performance, charging that "the
University lacks the physical, mental, and spiritual
leadership it demands."

632.   "Now, a Backlash on Campus Turmoil." *U.S. News and
World Report* 66 (10 March 1969): 10-11.

Excerpts from text of letter dated 24 February from
President Nixon to Hesburgh, following Hesburgh's
statement of expulsion for disruptive activity.
Includes excerpts of Hesburgh's letter to Vice-
President Agnew on 25 February 1969 which suggests
appropriate action in time of protest.

633.   O'Connor, John. "Hesburgh Fights." *Look* 33 (18
November 1969): 42.

634.   Payne, Thomas. "Come, Let Us Reason Together?"
Scholastic 110 (21 February 1969): 7.

Payne criticizes Hesburgh's letters on student
protests.

635.   _____. "Vox Alumni, Vox Dei." *Scholastic* 110
(28 February 1969): 10.

Quotes telegram from Robert Sam Anson, Class of '67,
to Hesburgh regarding student protests. Anson

suggests that Hesburgh resign.

636.   Steif, William. "Governor Reassured by Father
        Hesburgh and F.B.I. Veto Proposed Campus Inquiry."
        College and University Business 46 (April 1969): 79-
        80.

                          1970-1979

637.   "A New Portfolio." *Scholastic* 111 (16 January 1970): 4.

        Editorial criticizes Hesburgh: "We feel that the
        time has come that Father Hesburgh relinquish his
        office as president."--p. 4. Suggests a new administrative
        structure which accommodates positions of president
        and chancellor.

638.   Bayh, Birch. Dedication to Reverend Theodore M.
        Hesburgh, C.S.C. *Notre Dame Lawyer* 46 (Summer 1971):
        664-65.

        Bayh, United States Senator from Indiana, says of
        Hesburgh: "He has served as the irrepressible
        conscience of a divided and confused people and when
        something has needed to be said he has had the guts
        to say it . . . . He is both a staunch defender and
        stern critic of youth."--pp. 664-65.

639.   Brennan, William J., Jr. Dedication to Reverend
        Theodore M. Hesburgh, C.S.C. *Notre Dame Lawyer* 46
        (Summer 1971): 660-61.

        Brennan, associate justice, United States Supreme
        Court, considers Hesburgh "one of those rare persons
        who manage to do many things at the same time, and to
        excel in all of them. I think of his work in South
        and Central America, his participation in important
        international conferences on subjects of vital
        concern to the world, his special assignments for the

Vatican. Foremost for Americans, however, has been
his work with the Civil Rights Commission."--p. 660.

640.   Brewster, Kingman, Jr. Dedication to Reverend
Theodore M. Hesburgh, C.S.C. *Notre Dame Lawyer* 46
(Summer 1971): 668.

Brewster, president of Yale University, commends
Hesburgh on his ability to teach us how to be
outraged at the world's ills and injustices without
becoming sour.

641.   Cooke, Terence Cardinal. Dedication to Reverend
Theodore M. Hesburgh, C.S.C. *Notre Dame Lawyer* 46
(Summer 1971): 663.

Cooke praises Hesburgh as a man who has never lost
his sense of humor or his sense of values.

642.   Griswold, Erwin N. Dedication to Reverend Theodore M.
Hesburgh, C.S.C. *Notre Dame Lawyer* 46 (Summer 1971):
662-63.

Griswold, appointed to the U.S. Commission on Civil
Rights in 1961, praises Hesburgh for his "lasting
contribution to the moral tone of education . . . .
American legal education, and American law owe
him a profound debt."--p. 663.

643.   Hannah, John A. Dedication to Reverend Theodore M.
Hesburgh, C.S.C. *Notre Dame Lawyer* 46 (Summer 1971):
666-68.

Hannah, former chairman of the U.S. Commission on
Civil Rights, asserts that Hesburgh "has provided the
moral leadership which has made it possible for the
Commission to broaden its horizons and never to lose
sight of the fact that it is concerned not merely
with issues of law but with matters of conscience as
well."--p. 667. Hannah quotes in part Hesburgh's

statement in the Commission's 1961 Justice Report as one of Hesburgh's most eloquent expressions of his philosophy as a commissioner.

644. Johnson, Lyndon B. Dedication to Reverend Theodore M. Hesburgh, C.S.C. *Notre Dame Lawyer* 46 (Summer 1971): 659.

In 1964, President Johnson presented to Hesburgh the Medal of Freedom Award, the nation's highest honor, with the following citation: "Educator and humanitarian, he has inspired a generation of students and given of his wisdom in the struggle for the rights of man."--p. 659.

645. Lawless, William B. Dedication to Reverend Theodore M. Hesburgh, C.S.C. *Notre Dame Lawyer* 46 (Summer 1971): 661-62.

Lawless, Dean of the Notre Dame Law School (1968-1970), considers Hesburgh "chief architect of the most dynamic Catholic university in the world." Lawless states that the Notre Dame Law School will honor Hesburgh by "presently collecting all of the documents which he used and published as a member and chairman of the U.S. Civil Rights Commission."--p. 662.

646. "Letter from H. E. Cardinal Villot, Secretary of State, to Reverend Theodore M. Hesburgh." In *The Catholic University and Development,* by the International Federation of Catholic Universities, 13-15. Paris: Secrétariat Permanent de la F.I.U.C., 1971.

In a letter dated 19 August 1970 Villot, on behalf of the Holy Father, expresses his wish for Hesburgh's success as he presides over the Ninth General Assembly of the International Federation of Catholic Universities, Boston College, 26-29 August 1970.

"'Youth counts on you; know how to answer their
anxious and impatient waiting.'"--p. 15.

647. "Mellowing of a President." *Time* 97 (15 February
1971): 67.

Hesburgh's hard-line views on civil and local issues
have mellowed in the course of his career.

648. Rankin, Robert S. Dedication to Reverend Theodore M.
Hesburgh, C.S.C. *Notre Dame Lawyer* 46 (Summer 1971):
666.

Rankin, a member of the U.S. Commission on Civil
Rights, asserts that "Hesburgh's contributions to
the cause of civil rights have been far beyond measure
. . . . He has afforded the leadership that is so
necessary to any dynamic and forceful governmental
agency."--p. 666.

649. Stephan, Edmund A. Dedication to Reverend Theodore M.
Hesburgh, C.S.C. *Notre Dame Lawyer* 46 (Summer 1971):
666.

Stephan, then chairman of the Board of Trustees, University of Notre Dame, ranks Hesburgh as one of the
nation's "'public men'--those rare individuals who
have an instinctive grasp for the big issues of our
time, the intellectual equipment to deal with them
and the strength of character to move our society
towards a better life."--p. 666.

650. "A Tribute to Reverend Theodore M. Hesburgh, C.S.C."
by The Editors and Staff of the *Notre Dame Lawyer*.
Notre Dame Lawyer 46 (Summer 1971): 657-59.

In an issue dedicated to Hesburgh, a biographical
essay prepared by the editors and staff of *Notre Dame
Lawyer* outlines Hesburgh's life and distinguished
career. Includes portrait of Hesburgh in his prime.

651. Warren, Earl. Dedication to Reverend Theodore M.
      Hesburgh. *Notre Dame Lawyer* 46 (Summer 1971): 660.

      Warren, retired chief justice of the United States
      Supreme Court, lauds Hesburgh's monumental service
      to the nation in the cause of civil rights. "He has
      attacked with forthrightness and vigor the most
      divisive problem of American life--that of according
      civil rights to all Americans without regard to race
      or color. I believe that he and his fellow
      Commissioners have not been given the recognition
      they deserve for the arduous work they have per-
      formed."--p. 660.

652. Conklin, Richard W. "The Ecumenical Institute: N.D.'s
      Home in the Holy Land." *Notre Dame Magazine* 1
      (October 1972): 4-5.

      Background on the history and development of the
      Ecumenical Institute, Tantur, Jerusalem, which
      Hesburgh organized at the request of Pope Paul VI.

653. _____. "The Hesburgh Years: The Challenge of
      Change." *Notre Dame Magazine* 1 (June 1972): 13-17.

      A biographical essay on Hesburgh's life, noting his
      position on American higher education, civil rights,
      and issues in the institutional Church.

654. Connelly, Joel R. and Howard J. Dooley. "Hesburgh of
      Notre Dame: The Necessary Catholic." *Nation* 214
      (6 March 1972): 300-303.

      Reviews Hesburgh's accomplishments in transforming
      Notre Dame from a conservative "Catholic ghetto"
      to an institution recognized for academic excellence.

655. Deedy, John. "Ted in the Cabinet?" *Commonweal* 96
      (24 March 1972): 50.

Responds to Joel R. Connelly's article in *Nation*
(6 March 1972) which suggested that Hesburgh may be
in line for a cabinet-level position in the next
Administration.

656. Gilliam, Dorothy. "The Hesburgh Years: Civil Rights."
Notre Dame Magazine 1 (June 1972): 23-25.

The author, a former staff reporter for the *Washington
Post*, reviews the work of the U.S. Commission on
Civil Rights. Reprinted from *City, Magazine of
Urban Life and Environment*, January/February 1972.

657. Hughes, Tim. "Weathering the Faculty Storm." *Notre
Dame Magazine* 1 (June 1972): 26-29.

Discusses faculty dissent and letter sent to Hesburgh
concerning style of governance at the University, a
quota system for tenured faculty, and teaching loads.

658. "Law and Order and Father Hesburgh." *Christian
Century* 89 (6 December 1972): 1232-33.

Discusses Hesburgh's forced resignation from the U.S.
Civil Rights Commission which "not only exposes the
hypocrisy of the administration's 'commitment' to civil
rights, but also illumines the remarkable character
of the president of Notre Dame University .... His
commission has repeatedly embarrassed governmental
agencies charged with enforcing civil rights laws by
voicing public criticism of their policies, and he has
frequently spoken out against Nixon's antibusing
stand."--pp. 1232-33.

659. "Loss and Opportunity." *Commonweal* 97 (8 December
1972): 219-20.

Commentary on the ousting of Hesburgh from the
Civil Rights Commission, his extraordinary contributions in hard-core civil rights issues, and his

potential for further leadership in the American
Catholic Church.

660.   Shuster, George. "The Hesburgh Years: A Personal
Remembrance." *Notre Dame Magazine* 1 (June 1972):
19-21.

A lucid reflection on Hesburgh's career, focusing
on his leadership in the Church and confrontations
with student protesters in the late 1960's.

661.   Gleason, Philip. Review of *Hesburgh's Notre Dame:
Triumph in Transition*, by Joel R. Connelly and Howard
J. Dooley. *Notre Dame Magazine* 2 (February 1973):
48-49.

Gleason considers *Hesburgh's Notre Dame* "a student-
journalistic account of Notre Dame in the years from
1960-1972 . . . . In spite of the limitations inherent
in the approach adopted, the book has real value both
as a document and for the information it provides."
--p. 48.

662.   Hart, Philip A. "Notre Dame Law School Civil Rights
Lectures: Introduction." *Notre Dame Lawyer* 49
(October 1973): 5.

Lectures dedicated to Hesburgh delivered at the
Notre Dame Law School, 5-6 April 1973.

663.   "Memo to the White House." *Nation* 217 (3 December
1973): 580-81.

Hesburgh is quoted by *Nation's* editors as saying that
President Nixon is allowing the U.S. Civil Rights
Commission to "die on the vine."--p. 580.

664.   Shea, George W. Review of *Hesburgh's Notre Dame* by
Joel R. Connelly and Howard J. Dooley. *Commonweal* 98
(27 April 1973): 188-190.

Shea considers *Hesburgh's Notre Dame* "an unfortunate
book . . . written in slick magazine style by two recent
graduates who made no claim to serious historical
research."--p. 189.

665. Farrell, John J. "Disquieting Parallels." *Notre Dame
      Magazine* 3 (October 1974): 3.

      Farrell criticizes Hesburgh's remarks on poverty,
      racism, and abortion, as reported in *Notre Dame
      Magazine*, June 1974, pp. 21 ff.

666. Gresser, James. Review of *The Humane Imperative*, by
      Theodore M. Hesburgh. *Scholastic* 116 (22 November
      1974): 14.

      In a generally favorable review, Gresser commends
      Hesburgh's overview of imbalance examined from social,
      economic, political, and religious perspectives.

667. Mulcahey, Leo J. "People at ND." *Scholastic* 116
      (9 September 1974): 15.

      Hesburgh receives an honorary Bachelor of Arts degree
      at commencement exercises in May 1974. In 1937, his
      superiors sent him to Rome, two years shy of his
      graduation. Includes text of the whimsical citation.

668. "People at ND." *Scholastic* 115 (3 May 1974): 15.

      A *U.S. News and World Report* survey chose Hesburgh as
      one of the "most influential" leaders in the field of
      education.

669. "Hesburgh, Theodore M." In *Contemporary Authors*,
      edited by Clare D. Kinsman, 381-82. 1st revision,
      vols. 13-16. Detroit: Gale Research, 1975.

670. Kilian, Thomas J. "A Beef About the Food Crisis."
      Notre Dame Magazine 4 (June 1975): 3.

Kilian resents Hesburgh's statements published in his
article "Food in an Interdependent World" (*Notre Dame
Magazine*, April 1975, pp. 23-27) regarding beef and
the food crisis.

671.   Murphy, James E. "'Official Family' Discusses Future
of Notre Dame." *Notre Dame Magazine* 4 (October 1975):
4-5.

Discusses Hesburgh's meetings with 25 lay trustees in
a series of 14 meetings held during 1974 and 1975. One
key question: "Can we afford our vision?"

672.   Odem, Dave. "Feeding Livestock and People." *Notre
Dame Magazine* 4 (June 1975): 3.

Odem objects to some of Hesburgh's remarks on the food
crisis (*Notre Dame Magazine*, April 1975) as
"inaccurate, misleading and highly irresponsible."

673.   Payne, Thomas F. "Fable of the Spacecraft Earth II."
Notre Dame Magazine 4 (June 1975): 2-3.

Payne strongly criticizes Hesburgh's article on the
food crisis (*Notre Dame Magazine*, April 1975).

674.   Scharper, Philip. "Education Beyond the Schoolroom."
Review of *The Humane Imperative: A Challenge for the
Year 2000*, by Theodore M. Hesburgh. *America* 132
(25 January 1975): 53-54.

"If those who actually shape national and global
policy had time to read but one slender book . . . one
could passionately hope that it would be this one."--p. 54.

675.   "Speaker of the Year: Theodore M. Hesburgh." *Speaker
and Gavel* 12 (Summer 1975): 1.

Delta Sigma Rho-Tau Kappa Alpha, National Honorary
Forensic Society, selects Hesburgh as speaker of the

year because he has supported his positions with
reason and compassion, avoiding overstatement and
exaggeration.

676.   "Father Hesburgh's New Directions." *Notre Dame
Magazine* 5 (December 1976): 8-9.

Hesburgh, Norman Cousins, Robert McNamara, and
Margaret Mead form a new citizen's lobby called "New
Directions," organized to demonstrate America's
collective strength in world affairs. Carter appoints
Hesburgh as one of eleven persons to advise him on
major appointments in his administration.

677.   Ajemian, Robert I. "Prince of Priests, Without a
Nickel." *Time* 109 (2 May 1977): 74-75.

Outlines Hesburgh's public service career and his
attitudes on controversial issues.

678.   "Carter Keynotes Commencement." *Notre Dame Magazine*
6 (June 1977): 3.

Carter states Hesburgh "has spoken more consistently
and effectively in support of the rights of human
beings than any American I know . . . ." Includes
photograph.

679.   Sheedy, Charles E. "The Priest as President."
Notre Dame Magazine 6 (June 1977): 19-21.

Sheedy, Holy Cross priest and longtime friend of
Hesburgh, provides reliable biographical backdrop of
Hesburgh's life as priest and president. Includes
photographs.

680.   Leeper, E. M. "USA Readies Position for 1979 UN
Conference." *BioScience* 28 (February 1978): 85-87.

Discusses background and preparation for the U.N. Conference on Science and Technology for Development. Hesburgh considers the conference an opportunity to effect expansive changes which will be mutually beneficial to developing countries and to the U.S.

681.   "Annual Survey: Who Runs America?" *U.S. News and World Report* 86 (16 April 1979): 32-40.

Hesburgh ranks first as the most influential leader in religion, and second in education, following Joseph A. Califano, U.S. Secretary of Health, Education, and Welfare.

682.   Christopher, Michael. "On Being a Catholic President." *U.S. Catholic* 44 (October 1979): 48-51.

Christopher reflects on the Catholicity of John F. Kennedy and Hesburgh. He draws from two works: *John F. Kennedy: Catholic and Humanist* by Albert J. Menendez and *The Hesburgh Papers: Higher Values in Higher Education* by T. M. Hesburgh.

683.   Conklin, Dick. Review of *The Hesburgh Papers: Higher Values in Higher Education*, by Theodore M. Hesburgh. *Notre Dame Magazine* 8 (May 1979): 3.

Conklin provides background for the composition of *The Hesburgh Papers* which "contains the record of his educational philosophy--particularly his notion of the Catholic university and its place in society."

684.   "Hesburgh Leads Treaty Prayers." *Notre Dame Magazine* 8 (May 1979): 8.

Brief account of Hesburgh's address at an ecumenical service held at Washington's Lincoln Memorial, 26 March 1979 following the signing of the Israeli-Egyptian peace treaty.

685. "Hesburgh Tops Survey." *Christian Century* 96 (2 May 1979): 488.

The *U.S. News and World Report* annual survey on "Who Runs America" ranks Hesburgh first in religion and second in education among America's most influential decision-makers.

686. Kornegay, Francis Albert. "Comment." In *Equal Employment: Mandate and Challenge*, 173-75. New York: Vantage Press, 1979.

687. "The Lesson of Vienna." *Notre Dame Magazine* 8 (December 1979): 6.

Discusses the results of the U.N. Conference on Science and Technology in Vienna. James Grant, executive director of UNICEF, attributed much of the success to U.S. Ambassador Hesburgh, who recognized injustice between nations and peoples and urged action in lieu of argument.

688. McInnes, William. Review of *The Hesburgh Papers: Higher Values in Higher Education*, by Theodore M. Hesburgh. *America* 140 (26 May 1979): 438.

McInnes objects that some of Hesburgh's essays were prepared to be heard, not read, for past rather than contemporary audiences.

689. Zelenko, Barbara. Review of *The Hesburgh Papers: Higher Values in Higher Education*, by Theodore M. Hesburgh. *Library Journal* 104 (15 June 1979): 1334.

Zelenko criticizes Hesburgh's segment on campus unrest as dated. She considers some essays valuable for their practicality, but most she considers too lofty for exciting reading.

1980-1988

690. Kerr, Clark. Review of *The Hesburgh Papers: Higher Values in Higher Education,* by Theodore M. Hesburgh. *Journal of Higher Education* 51 (1980): 566-68.

Kerr offers high praise on Hesburgh's work, calling him the conscience of higher education and civil rights for the nation.

691. Zuehlke, Gus. "A Call to Eucharist." *Scholastic* 122 (December 1980): 6-7.

Zuehlke's article describes Hesburgh's dedication to the daily celebration of the Eucharist. Hesburgh's fundamental vision flows from his participation in the mystery of the Eucharistic sacrifice. Given a choice, he would rather celebrate the Eucharist than be president of the United States.

692. "Chancellor Hesburgh? The Trustees Split the Administration." *Notre Dame Magazine* 10 (July 1981): 3.

"Notre Dame's Board of Trustees has created the position of chancellor at the University, and it is expected that Father Hesburgh will assume that role when he steps down in the spring of 1982." Discusses plans for administrative changes which include a "top management team."

693. "Encore! Father Hesburgh Agrees to Five More Years." *Notre Dame Magazine* 10 (December 1981): 3-5.

Edmund A. Stephan, chairman of the Notre Dame Board of Trustees, declares Notre Dame should not change leadership given Hesburgh's excellent record and vitality. Four Holy Cross priests are appointed to upper level administrative positions: Ernest Bartell, William Beauchamp, Edward A. Malloy, and

David T. Tyson.

694. "Father Hesburgh." *America* 145 (10 October 1981): 191.

Notice of Hesburgh's impending retirement. The American Council on Education plans to grant him its second annual award for leadership.

695. "A Guide for Notre Dame's Next President." *Notre Dame Magazine* 10 (May 1981): 5.

Hesburgh requests Provost Timothy O'Meara to produce the PACE (Priorities and Commitments for Excellence) report, which "will be the final document of the Hesburgh years and will serve as a guide for Notre Dame's next president."

696. "Minor Planet Named After Hesburgh." *Notre Dame Report* 10 (6 February 1981): 313.

"A minor planet, discovered May 3, 1951, at the Goethe Link Observatory at Indiana University, has been named in honor of Rev. Theodore M. Hesburgh . . . . Hesburgh, the planet, was listed for the first time this January in the Minor Planet Circulars which cited Hesburgh, the priest, for his 'extraordinary record of public service in areas ranging from the humanitarian to the technical and scientific.'" --p. 313. During his twelve year term as a member of the National Science Board, Hesburgh played an important role in the founding of the Kitt Peak National Observatory, Tucson, Arizona, and the Cerro Tololo Interamerican Observatory (CTIO) in La Serena, Chile.

697. "On File." *Origins* 10 (19 February 1981): 562.

Hesburgh announces plans to retire in the spring of 1982. His successor must be a priest from the Indiana

Province of the Congregation of the Holy Cross.

698.   "On File." *Origins* 11 (5 November 1981): 326.

Acceding to the request of the University Board of Trustees, Hesburgh agrees to remain as university president for another five years.

699.   "Opening the Golden Door." *Commonweal* 108 (13 February 1981): 67-68.

Editorial supports Hesburgh's position on immigration reform which advocates worker identification and employer sanctions.

700.   Brashler, William. "The Indispensable Man." *Notre Dame Magazine* 11 (May 1982): 36-38.

An article on the life of Edmund Stephan, retiring chairman of the Notre Dame Board of Trustees, discusses briefly Hesburgh's enduring relationship with Stephan, one of his closest friends.

701.   Conn, Charles Paul. "Our Modern Patriots." *Saturday Evening Post* 254 (July-August 1982): 50-55; 124.

Describes Hesburgh's career and his active participation in national affairs.

702.   "Hesburgh, Theodore Martin." In *Current Biography Yearbook 1982*, edited by Charles Moritz, 155-58. New York: H. W. Wilson, 1982.

Although somewhat dated, one of the best biographical sketches of its kind on Hesburgh's career.

703.   Conklin, Richard W. "A Reminder in Vienna." *Notre Dame Magazine* 12 (May 1983): 26-27.

Conklin, serving as a press officer at the Vienna conference on nuclear war, provides background information on Hesburgh's meetings in Vienna in 1981, 1982, and 1983 during which Hesburgh launched his extraordinary private initiative for peace.

704.   "On File." *Origins* 12 (6 January 1983): 474.

Hesburgh named member of the Pontifical Council for Culture.

705.   Pfaff, William. "The Hesburgh Initiative." *Notre Dame Magazine* 12 (May 1983): 22-25.

A detailed essay describing Hesburgh's initiative to effect a mutual reduction of nuclear arms. "The Hesburgh plea, like the American bishops' draft statement on nuclear war, expresses a reaction to the administration's emphasis on nuclear buildup, war fighting, and the 'immorality' of the Soviet system. It is designed to 'raise consciousness,' as Father Hesburgh repeatedly says."--p. 25.

706.   Underwood, John. "Casting a Special Light: A Critic of Colleges That Stoop Academically to Conquer Athletically Sees in Notre Dame--and Its Two Enduring Leaders--Much Worth Emulating." *Sports Illustrated* 58 (10 January 1983): 58-62; 64; 66-70.

"In recent years, Hesburgh and Joyce have been outspoken critics of those abuses that have fouled college sports."--p. 64.

707.   "Father Theodore M. Hesburgh." In *Biographies: God at Their Sides,* edited by Francis Heerey, 63-66. New York: Regina Press, 1984.

A brief biographical sketch of Hesburgh written for children and young adults. Mentions Hesburgh's ten-point program, adopted in 1953, enabling collegiate football games to be televised.

708. "'To Move Mountains for Peace.'" *Notre Dame Magazine*
13 (Summer 1984): 13.

At Notre Dame's 139th commencement, Provost Timothy
O'Meara surprises Hesburgh with his 100th honorary
degree, declaring him "'a man of complex simplicity,
unswerving faith and tireless leadership.'"

709. Underwood, John. "A Shining Example." In *Spoiled
Sport: A Fan's Notes on the Troubles of Spectator
Sports*, 235-71. Boston: Little, Brown, 1984.

In a chapter which highlights the history of Notre
Dame's leading football figures, Underwood discusses
the influence of Hesburgh and Joyce.

710. Griffin, Robert F. "Facing Life Without Father."
Notre Dame Magazine 14 (Spring 1985): 11.

Hesburgh's leadership at Notre Dame has shown
students the value of service and world citizenship.

711. Woodward, Kenneth L. "Rome's New School Rules."
Newsweek 106 (11 November 1985): 82.

Discussion of the draft directive, issued in April
1985 by the Vatican's Sacred Congregation for
Catholic Education, stating that no Catholic university
can consider itself "a purely private institution."

712. "Campus Leaders." *Touchdown Illustrated Magazine* 22
(8 November 1986): 14-16.

Profiles Edmund P. Joyce and Hesburgh as they enter
their 35th year of service. During their leadership,
alumni support at Notre Dame has ranked among the
highest in the nation.

713. Conklin, Richard. "A Modest Proposal? The Vatican
      Challenges Catholic Academia's Declaration of
      Independence." *Notre Dame Magazine* 15 (Summer 1986):
      7-8.

      Conklin provides an excellent summary and synthesis
      of the heated debate over the "Proposed Schema for a
      Pontifical Document on Catholic Universities." He
      describes Hesburgh's vital role in forming the
      Land O'Lakes Statement in 1967 and states clearly
      Hesburgh's critique of the proposed Schema.

714. Doyle, Joe. "Looking Back at Father Ted." *Touchdown
      Illustrated Magazine* 22 (15 November 1986): 149-51.

      In an illustrated article appearing in the Notre
      Dame-Penn State football program, sports editor Joe
      Doyle offers a warm personal reflection of his
      friendship with Father Ted which began in the spring
      of 1946.

715. "Home Again." *Notre Dame Magazine* 14 (Winter 1985-
      1986): 13.

      Near Notre Dame's Grotto, Hesburgh and Joyce dedicate
      a bronze sculpture of Tom Dooley with two Laotian
      children.

716. Lipo, Frank. "The End of an Era." *Scholastic* 128
      (2 October 1986): 10-11.

      Biographical account of Hesburgh's career, highlight-
      ing the growth of the university under Hesburgh's
      administration.

717. Peralta, Elizabeth. "To Pick a President." *Notre Dame
      Magazine* 15 (Spring 1986): 3-4.

      Peralta describes the process of selecting Hesburgh's
      successor. Hesburgh expresses concern over the

Vatican's attempt to provide guidelines for defining
a Catholic university.

718.   Schmuhl, Robert P. "Profile: Rev. Theodore M.
Hesburgh, C.S.C., University President." In
University of Notre Dame: A Contemporary Portrait, by
Robert Schmuhl, 18-25. Notre Dame, Ind.: University
of Notre Dame Press, 1986.

Schmuhl presents a balanced and thorough account of
Hesburgh's achievements during his thirty-five year
presidency at Notre Dame. The major accomplishments
of Hesburgh's life and the impact of his leadership
are rendered in an accurate, well-written essay.

719.   Temple, Kerry. "Waiting in the Wings." *Notre Dame
Magazine* 15 (Summer 1986): 5-6.

Temple discusses Hesburgh's career as president, and
profiles five potential successors: Thomas Oddo,
Ernest Bartell; William Beauchamp; Edward Malloy; and
David Tyson.

720.   Bacard, André. "Sparking Life into Our Youth."
Humanist 47 (July/August 1987): 46.

Refers to Hesburgh's proposal that we institutionalize the Peace Corps as we have done with the ROTC.
With scholarships awarded to Peace Corps candidates,
students could study the culture, politics and the
language of areas in which they wished to serve.
Upon graduation, they would then fulfill four years
in public service abroad.

721.   Bowen, Ezra. "His Trumpet Was Never Uncertain:
Hesburgh Retires from Notre Dame After 35 Years."
Time 129 (18 May 1987): 68-71.

Discusses in detail the more important aspects of
Hesburgh's career and his forthcoming retirement.

Hesburgh equates the essence of leadership with vision: "You can't blow an uncertain trumpet."--p. 68.

722.   "First in His Class." *Commonweal* 114 (5 June 1987): 341-42.

"Hesburgh has shaped a university where Catholic faith, values, and commitment are cultivated as well as academic competence, and where freedom of inquiry is insured for both students and faculty."--p. 342.

723.   Gleason, Philip. "The More Things Change." *Notre Dame Magazine* 15 (Winter 1986-1987): 8-9.

Gleason provides a valuable and seasoned historical account of continuity and change at Notre Dame during the Hesburgh era, with particular attention to the issue of Notre Dame's Catholic identity during thirty-five years of Hesburgh leadership.

724.   Hechinger, Fred. "A Servant of Church and Academe." *Notre Dame Magazine* 16 (Spring 1987): 15-21.

Highlights Hesburgh's career, including his involvement with Nixon during the student protests of 1969, his role as champion of civil rights, the creation of the Institute for Peace Studies, and his concern for quality in Catholic education.

725.   "Hesburgh, Theodore Martin." In *Who's Who in America, 1986-1987*. 44th ed., vol. 1, 1271-72. Chicago: Marquis Who's Who, 1987.

This and previous editions list concise biographical information on Hesburgh's background and career.

726.   Hunt, George W. "Father Hesburgh Retires." *America* 156 (30 May 1987): 433.

Hesburgh's story "illustrates the way a religious order brings a community's gifts and institutional continuity to the service of both the church and the whole human family."--p. 433.

727.	_____. "Of Many Things." Review of *Hesburgh of Notre Dame*, by John C. Lungren. *America* (30 May 1987): Inside front cover.

Brief laudatory review of Lungren's *Hesburgh of Notre Dame*. Commends Hesburgh's strength of character in expediting the release of Robert Sam Anson, a former Notre Dame student, who was held prisoner of war in Cambodia. In 1969, Anson suggested to Hesburgh that he resign.

728.	Leclercq, Georges. "A Tribute to Father Hesburgh." *News in Brief* 64 (November 1987): 2-3.

Leclercq, former Rector of the Catholic University of Lille, recalls Hesburgh's incredible strength as president of the International Federation of Catholic Universities, particularly during periods of intense confrontation.

729.	Lungren, John C., Jr., "They'll Probably Appoint Some Rabbit in My Place." *Notre Dame Magazine* 16 (Spring 1987): 20-21.

Adapted from Lungren's book *Hesburgh of Notre Dame: Priest, Educator, Public Servant*, 1987. Highlights Nixon's call in 1972 for Hesburgh's resignation from the Civil Rights Commission.

730.	"Notre Dame's Hesburgh Defies Nuclear 'Insanity,' June 7, 1984." In *The Paper Sword of Bill Rentschler*, by William H. Rentschler, 69-71. Chicago: Chicago Review Press, 1987.

731. Schaal, Carol. "Twilight of a Presidency." *Notre Dame Magazine* 16 (Summer 1987): 6.

In retirement, Hesburgh hopes to continue his work by fund raising, writing, and involvement in campus affairs.

732. "The Time for Parting." *Notre Dame Magazine* 15 (Summer 1987): 14.

Describes Hesburgh's final commencement as president of the University of Notre Dame. Hesburgh became the first Holy Cross priest to receive the Laetare Medal, the University's highest honor.

733. Walsh, Catherine. "Father Theodore Hesburgh." *St. Anthony Messenger* 94 (May 1987): 28-34.

A biographical account of Hesburgh's career as citizen of the church and the world. Discusses academic freedom and the Vatican Schema.

734. Whitehead, Kenneth D. "Religiously Affiliated Colleges and American Freedom." *America* (7 February 1987): 41-43.

Alludes to Hesburgh's article "Catholic Education in America" (*America*, 4 October 1986) and discusses the question of academic freedom.

735. Woodward, Kenneth L. "Notre Dame's 'Father Ted' Bids Farewell." *Newsweek* 109 (11 May 1987): 75 ff.

Reviews Hesburgh's presidency and his plans to continue working toward world peace.

736. Wulf, Steve. "Fathers Ted and Ed." *Sports Illustrated* 66 (25 May 1987): 17.

Describes the careers of Hesburgh and Joyce as they
retire from the helm.

737. Cockburn, Alexander. "An Odious Fellow." *Nation*
247 (16/23 July 1988): 45.

Cockburn criticizes Hesburgh on several accounts,
citing incidents and issues concerning the Vietnam
War, student protests, unionization, divestment in
South Africa, minorities, and women's rights.

738. _____. "Shell Games: Further Adventures of the
Odious Fellow." *Nation* 247 (10 October 1988):
300-301.

Cockburn alludes to Hesburgh in regard to the contro-
versy over the proposed Institute for the Study of Post-
Apartheid Problems at Notre Dame. Peter Walshe, a
Notre Dame professor "who has reported the collusion
between the university and Shell in *Common Sense*,
an alternative campus paper, says negotiations are
now under way for a Shell-sponsored institute at the
school. In other words, the University of Notre Dame,
which has a declared policy of not cooperating with
firms supplying South Africa's military and police
forces, is about to assist both Shell and the apartheid
regime in their P.R. stratagems."--301.

739. "A Counter ROTC." *Christian Century* 105 (20 January
1988): 48.

Discusses the Hesburgh-Pell legislation, endorsed by
Loret Miller Ruppe, head of the Peace Corps, calling
for a government-funded "peace-equivalent" to ROTC
military training programs in colleges and universities.
Hesburgh proposed the plan and Senator Claiborne Pell
(D., R.I.) is sponsoring the legislation which provides
education and living expenses for college juniors and
seniors interested in working on peace and development
projects overseas.

740. Garvey, Michael. ""Hesburgh Participates in
International Human Rights Conference." *Notre
Dame Basketball* (21 January 1988): 64.

Hesburgh, instrumental in initiatives to eliminate
nuclear weapons, joined more than forty participants
at a conference on human rights held 4-6 January 1988
in The Netherlands. Issues discussed included freedom
of thought, conscience and religious belief, and
freedom of movement across international boundaries.

741. "Rev. Theodore M. Hesburgh, C.S.C." *Notre Dame Report*
18 (4 November 1988): 111.

Report of Hesburgh's participation in a conference
sponsored by the International Association of
Universities, Tallories, France, to organize an
effort for disarmament through education. Recommendations included "the development of a new inter-
disciplinary curriculum to address arms control
and negotiation, university support for scholars and
courses focusing on arms control and conflict
management, and the development of international
information centers."

742. Robinson, James A. "Lieutenants to Learning: A
Bibliography of Participant-Observation by University
Presidents." *Journal of Higher Education* 59 (May/
June 1988): 327-51.

Robinson, president of the University of West Florida,
presents an essay and bibliography of books of more
than one hundred chief executive officers of colleges
and universities written during or after their tenure.
He cites two works by Hesburgh, and notes that
"Notre Dame's Father Hesburgh (1979), whose charity for
others must be nearly as boundless as his religion
requires, counsels presidents never to expect thanks
for their good works."--p. 330.

743. Townley, Roderick. "TV Will Always Expose the
     Phonies." *TV Guide* 37 (7 January 1989): 48-50.

     Townley reports on Hesburgh's attitudes toward
     television and his interest in teleconferencing.
     Hesburgh estimates he has spent about 1000 hours
     appearing on television, frequently on interview
     shows. He considers the misuse of television quite
     dangerous, especially for the young who may be out
     of touch with great books.

Newspaper Articles About Theodore M. Hesburgh

744. "Native of Syracuse to Head Notre Dame." *New York Times*, 28 June 1952, p. 17.

   Brief notice of Hesburgh's appointment as fifteenth president of Notre Dame, succeeding Rev. John J. Cavanaugh, C.S.C.

745. "Notre Dame President Visits Parents Here." *Syracuse Herald-American*, 28 December, 1952. UNDA: UDIS-Biographical Files.

   Brief article and photograph of Hesburgh with his parents, family, and friends before attending the annual holiday ball of the Central New York Club at the Bellevue Country Club.

746. "65 at Notre Dame Criticized." *New York Times*, 30 October 1952, p. 27.

   Quotes in part Hesburgh's statement criticizing 65 faculty members at Notre Dame who avowed their support of Gov. Adlai E. Stevenson, Democratic candidate for president. Hesburgh asserted that their action jeopardized the nonpartisan position of the university.

747. Lewis, Anthony. "Eisenhower Picks Civil Rights Unit; Reed is Chairman." *New York Times*, 8 November 1957.

1960-1969

748. "Hesburgh Named by JFK to Advisory Commission." *South Bend Tribune*, 4 April 1962.

President Kennedy appoints Hesburgh to the U.S. Advisory Commission on International Education and Internal Affairs.

749. Colwell, Jack. "Father Theodore M. Hesburgh, C.S.C.: He Moved the Golden Dome." *South Bend Tribune Magazine*, 3 May, 1964.

Entire issue devoted to Hesburgh and Notre Dame.

750. "Notre Dame President to Get K. of C. Award." *Chicago Tribune*, 12 March 1965.

Hesburgh named recipient of the 1965 Lantern Award from the Massachusetts Knights of Columbus in recognition of outstanding service to God and country.

751. "Students Pay Tribute to Hesburgh: Over 800 Attend Testimonial Dinner." *South Bend Tribune*, 29 April 1965.

Includes photograph of oil portrait of Hesburgh done by John Bellamy, senior fine arts major.

752. "University of Vienna Honors Father Hesburgh: Honorary Citizen." *Our Sunday Visitor*, 9 May 1965.

753. "*Clip Sheet: University of Notre Dame News*. Notre Dame, Ind.: Department of Public Relations and Information, University of Notre Dame, 1968-

UNDA; UDIS.

Clip Sheet, a compilation of articles from local and
national newspapers and periodicals, provides news which
relates to Notre Dame faculty, students, and/or
alumni. This service, prepared and distributed by
the Department of Public Relations and Information,
offers a convenient source of information for
articles by and about Hesburgh.

754. "Academic Freedom Document Presented." *Register*,
1 June 1969. UNDA: UDIS-Biographical Files.

Hesburgh presents a position paper to the Congregation
for Catholic Education in Rome strongly endorsing
autonomy and academic freedom at Catholic colleges
and universities.

755. Fleming, T. J. "Hesburgh of Notre Dame--(1) He's
Destroying the University; (2) He's Bringing It into
the Mainstream of American Life." *New York Times
Magazine*, 11 May 1969, pp. 56-57ff.

756. "Fr. Hesburgh Outlines National Youth Program." *St.
Louis Review*, 6 June 1969. UNDA.

Contains a detailed description of Hesburgh's four-
point program for youth.

1970-1979

757. "Fighting for Equal Rights: Theodore Martin
Hesburgh." *New York Times*, 11 June 1971, p. 12.

Highlights the indictment of the Federal Housing
Commission by the U.S. Commission on Civil Rights,
which Hesburgh chaired.

758. "Busing a Phony Issue Notre Dame President Tells Stonehill Group." *Brockton Enterprise and Brockton Times*, 30 May 1972. UNDA.

759. "Fr. Hesburgh at Stonehill Graduation." *The Anchor* (Diocese of Fall River, Mass.), 1 June 1972. UNDA.

760. "Two Farewells to Father Hesburgh." Albert S. Pacetta, Paul Moore, Jr. *New York Times*, 7 December 1972.

    Two distinctly opposite views of Hesburgh which focus on his role and resignation from the U.S. Civil Rights Commission.

761. "A 'Declaration of Independence' Needed for U.S. Bicentennial." *Catholic Messenger* (Davenport, Ia.), 13 February 1975, p. 3.

    Report on Hesburgh's address to the U.S. bishops at a bicentennial celebration in Washington, D.C.

762. Casucci, Pat. "New Group to Lobby for Peace, Justice, Says Fr. Hesburgh." *Catholic Herald Citizen* (Madison, Wis., ed.), 30 October 1976.

    At the bicentennial observance at Beloit College on 14 October 1976 Hesburgh reveals the establishment of New Directions, a forum for international problems which he launched with Margaret Mead and others.

763. Eddy, Jack. "Death Penalty Argued." *Beloit Daily News*, 15 October 1976.

    During an open forum at Beloit College, Hesburgh stresses opposition to the death penalty as a deterrent to crime. U.S. Attorney General Edward Levi takes an opposite stance.

764. Robinson, Gail. "CNR Graduates 800; Speaker Warns
Against Pessimism." *Standard-Star* (New Rochelle,
N.Y.), 24 May 1976.

Report of Hesburgh's commencement address to the
graduates of the College of New Rochelle on 23 May
1976 in which he traces the growth of human rights
in the United States.

765. Maeroff, Gene I. "Hesburgh Has Transformed Notre Dame
in His 25 Years." *New York Times*, 23 May 1977, p. 13.

Hesburgh hosts President Carter as commencement
speaker.

766. Cross, Robert. "Priest, College President, Citizen of
the World: The Rev. Theodore Hesburgh of Notre Dame
Fills All Three Roles, and He Does So With Energy,
Grace, and Compassion." *Chicago Tribune Magazine*, 12
November 1978, sec. 9, pp. 30-31ff.

Biographical article on Hesburgh, tracing his early
life, education, administrative accomplishments,
concern for academic excellence, and involvement in
civil rights. Discusses Land O' Lakes statement which
ensured that Catholic universities would retain true
autonomy and academic freedom.

1980-1988

767. Krebs, Albin and Judith Cummings. "Hesburgh on
Cambodia." *New York Times*, 12 September 1980, p. 10.

768. Barbour, John. "Hesburgh: He Controls the Quality."
South Bend Tribune, 10 May 1981.

769. "Father Hesburgh Decries Humanities De-emphasis."
News From Hope College (Holland, Mich.), 1 October
1981. UNDA.

Delivering the opening convocation address for Hope's academic year, Hesburgh says liberal education "must be characterized first of all by attention to ends rather than means, to substance rather than to process, to *being* human first and foremost, and then doing humanely . . . ."

770. "Hesburgh to Return Next Year." *New York Times*, 15 February 1981, sec. 1, p. 16.

771. Krebs, Albin, and Robert McG. Thomas, Jr. "Notre Dame's Talent Search That Ended at Home." *New York Times*, 26 October 1981, Late edition, p. B10.

772. Hechinger, Fred M. "About Education: Leadership Arises as a College Issue." *New York Times*, 19 October 1982.

The Council for Advancement and Support of Education awards the Jefferson Medal to Hesburgh, citing his role in university leadership by being "Father Ted" to generations of students, playing a key role in civil rights, combating world hunger, and working for worldwide nuclear disarmament.

773. Ingalls, Zoe. "For God, For Country and For Notre Dame." *Chronicle of Higher Education*, 13 October 1982, pp. 4-7.

Extensive coverage of Hesburgh's career, awards, management style, and drive for academic excellence.

774. Marcin, Joe. "Father Ted Speaks Out." *Sporting News*, 20 December 1982, p. 34.

Hesburgh advocates plan to ensure academic standards among college athletes.

775. Savitskas, Charles Anthony, Jr. "Hope Seems Distant in Witch's Broth of El Salvador." *Our Sunday*

Visitor, 27 June 1982, p. 6.

776. "$25,000 Grants for Papers of Vance and Hesburgh."
      New York Times, 1 November 1982, Late edition, p. 18.

777. Mitchell, William J. "Hesburgh: A 'Cocky' Longshot."
      National Catholic Reporter, 28 January 1983, p. 8.

      In a news analysis, Mitchell discusses Hesburgh's
      involvement with scientific and religious leaders in
      Vienna, and Hesburgh's deep concern with the cause of
      arms control. "Hesburgh is sharply critical of
      Reagan's policy of nuclear deterence . . . ."--p. 8.

778. Peralta, Elizabeth. "The Significant Tradition at
      Notre Dame." *Today in Michiana* 4 (October 1983): 22-
      26.

      Illustrated biographical account of Hesburgh's
      career.

779. Farrell, Michael J. "Most Honored Doctor in the
      History of the World." *National Catholic Reporter*,
      22 March 1985, p. 28.

780. "Notre Dame Rejects Stocks Divestment Tide."
      National Catholic Register, 10 November 1985, p. 2.

781. "Hesburgh Collapses at Yale." *South Bend Tribune*,
      21 September 1986.

      Hesburgh is admitted to Yale-New Haven Hospital in
      stable condition after a "fainting episode."

782. "Hesburgh Quits Hospital After Fainting Spell." *New
      York Times*, 22 September 1986, Late edition, p. B4.

783. Higgins, George C. "Father Hesburgh: Public Servant."
      Tidings, 24 October 1986.

220   Theodore M. Hesburgh

Highlights Hesburgh's career as chairman of Civil Rights Commission and chairman of Select Commission on Immigration and Refugee Policy.

784. McBrien, Richard. "He's One of Our Proudest Boasts." *Catholic Messenger*, 13 November 1986.

McBrien, noted Notre Dame theologian, offers an assessment of Hesburgh's stature, influence, and leadership.

785. "Notre Dame President Makes Good With Peers." *USA Today*, 31 October 1986.

James Fisher and Martha Tack, Bowling Green State University, surveyed 485 academics to pick the most effective presidents. Hesburgh "was named the USA's most effective" president.

786. Spencer, Jim, and Bruce Buursma. "Reaching for Greatness." *Chicago Tribune Magazine*, 9 November 1986, p. 10ff.

Detailed article providing insight into Hesburgh's personality, professional achievements, and lifestyle. "The concept of the Peace Institute is the essence of Hesburgh's idea of what higher education ought to be-- an ability to mix faith and scholarship and come up with something that is both intellectually satisfying and morally sound."--p. 2.

787. Walshe, Peter. "Notre Dame Dollars for Apartheid: Hesburgh Defies Disinvestment." *National Catholic Reporter*, 2 May 1986, p. 9.

788. Berkow, Ira. "Touchdown for Father Ted." *New York Times*, 14 May 1987, Late edition, p. D28.

"Hesburgh has overseen a sports program that many consider a model: one with integrity in recruiting,

with graduating its athletes, and with producing
competitive--though not necessarily undefeated--
teams."--p. D28.

789.   Brelis, Matthew. "A Call to Lead: Educate the Poor,
       Hesburgh Says in Pitt Speech." *Pittsburgh Press*,
       11 May 1987.

       Hesburgh urges urban universities to assume roles of
       leadership in educating the poor to prevent America
       from becoming a second-rate nation.

790.   Briggs, Kenneth. "Hesburgh's N.D. Leadership Ends
       After 35 Years." *National Catholic Reporter*, 22 May
       1987.

       An extensive summary and analysis of Hesburgh's
       career. On matters of church doctrine, particularly
       sexuality, "Hesburgh has been virtually silent."

791.   "Father Hesburgh Prepares His Valedictory." *Chronicle
       of Higher Education*, 13 May 1987.

       Comments on Hesburgh's valedictory address and his
       efforts to transform Notre Dame into a great Catholic
       university.

792.   "Father Hesburgh to Receive N.D. Laetare Medal."
       Today's Catholic, 12 April 1987.

793.   Gould, Herb. "Hesburgh Detached and Attached to
       Irish." *Chicago Sun Times*, 2 August 1987.

       Hesburgh explains why he declines addressing athletic
       gatherings.

794.   Hays, Charlotte. "Notre Dame: Is There Life After
       Hesburgh? Edward Malloy Will Find Out." *National
       Catholic Register*, 17 May 1987.

Views of Hesburgh's Notre Dame by several Notre Dame faculty, including Timothy O'Meara, Marvin O'Connell and J. Philip Gleason who comment on the Catholic identity of the university.

795.   "The Hesburgh Legend." Editorial. *New York Times*, 22 May 1987, Late edition, p. A30.

"His most radical move was to bring coeducation to a male bastion. His most important was to cede control of Notre Dame to a lay board of trustees. That way, he explained, the school would be assured of remaining both Catholic and free."--p. A30.

796.   "Hesburgh Warns Colleges to 'Clean Up' Acts." *South Bend Tribune*, 11 December 1987.

Hesburgh cites Heisman Trophy winner Tim Brown as an exemplary college athlete. He endorses the proposal made by Rev. Edmund P. Joyce at the College Football Association.

797.   "The Hesburgh Years." *Observer*, Special Issue, Spring 1987. 52 pp.

Entire issue includes a series of articles and tributes to Hesburgh and Joyce in honor of their thirty-five years at Notre Dame.

798.   Hinchion, Gail. "Hesburgh: Retiring N.D. Leader Leaves Golden Legacy. *South Bend Tribune*, 17 May 1987, A1, A12-13.

799.   _____. "Hesburgh Accomplishments During Career Nearly Outshine Golden Dome." *South Bend Tribune*, 17 May 1987, A13.

Fernand Dutile, Frederick Crosson, and Derek Bok comment on Hesburgh's achievements and accessibility.

800. Ingalls, Zoe. "Father Hesburgh Prepares His
      Valedictory." *Chronicle of Higher Education*, 13 May
      1987, p. 3.

801. Johnson, Dirk. "After 35 Years as President, Hesburgh
      Retires." *New York Times*, 18 May 1987, Late edition,
      p. B6.

      Derek C. Bok, president of Harvard University,
      delivered the keynote address at Hesburgh's last
      commencement ceremony as president of the University of
      Notre Dame. In taking leave, Hesburgh declared "there
      are battles yet to be won for justice--mountains to be
      climbed to overcome prejudice, ignorance, even
      stupidity."

802. Keough, Donald. Tribute to Hesburgh. *Observer*,
      Special Issue, Spring 1987.

      In honoring Hesburgh, Keough, chairman of the
      Notre Dame Board of Trustees, pays lasting and
      enlightened tribute to Hesburgh as priest and
      mediator.

803. "Library, ACC Are Renamed." *South Bend Tribune*,
      12 May 1987.

      Notre Dame's Memorial Library and the Athletic and
      Convocation Center are renamed in honor of Theodore
      M. Hesburgh and Edmund P. Joyce respectively.

804. McCarthy, Colman. "Hesburgh's Notre Dame." *Washington
      Post*, 9 May 1987, p. A23.

805. Morriss, Frank. "Why No Truly Catholic Leadership
      Comes from Notre Dame." *The Wanderer*, 30 July 1987.

      Morriss, critical of Hesburgh, states that the
      university "has not produced real Catholic leader-
      ship." Morriss equates Catholic leadership with

papal loyalty and questions some of Hesburgh's ideas
and attitudes.

806. "Notre Dame Grads Recall Influence of Rev. Hesburgh."
      Indianapolis Star, 24 May 1987.

      Mike Ahern, Romano L. Mazzoli, and Bruce E. Babbitt,
      former governor of Arizona, reflect on Hesburgh's
      influence upon their lives with T.V. host Phil Donahue.

807. "Notre Dame Sets Fund Drive as Hesburgh Says
      Goodbye." *New York Times,* 10 May 1987, sec. 1, p. 24.

808. Sniadecki, Rod. "N.D. Opens Tennis Pavilion." *South
      Bend Tribune,* 11 June 1987.

      Hesburgh dedicates the Eck Pavilion, gift of Mr. and
      Mrs. Franklin E. Eck of Columbus, Ohio.

809. Storch, Niel T. "Catholic Universities Are Facing an
      Academic Freedom Dilemma." *Chronicle of Higher
      Education,* 30 September 1987.

      Discusses Hesburgh's crucial role in attempting to
      define the relationship between church authority and
      theological inquiry.

810. Walshe, Peter. "The Hesburgh Legacy." *Common Sense,*
      April/May 1987.

      Walshe credits Hesburgh's defense of academic
      freedom in a Catholic context as his "pre-eminent
      achievement." He criticizes Hesburgh's position on
      divestment in South Africa.

811. Estabrook, Carl G. "On Benefaction; Or, Ted and the
      Notre Dame Ten." *Common Sense,* February 1988, p.
      1 ff.

Estabrook discusses "'The Notre Dame Ten--ten students condemned by the University authorities and rusticated for their violations of good order in the academic year 1969-70.'--p. 1. With reference to Hesburgh's comment that he is in the "pardoning business" for Vietnam draft resisters, Estabrook states that it is "as revealing as it is nauseating, combining as it does bad theology of a clericalist sort with a capitalist metaphor that would make John Tetzel blush."--p. 6.

812.   "Father Hesburgh Saluted for Humanitarian Efforts." *AFL-CIO News*, 25 June 1988, p. 1.

In New Orleans, the AFL-CIO grants Hesburgh the Murray-Green-Meany Award, the federation's highest tribute for humanitarianism.

813.   "Hesburgh Calls on Colleges to Influence U.S. Culture." *Today's Catholic*, 5 June 1988, p. 7.

At a meeting cosponsored by the Association of Catholic Colleges and Universities and the Pontifical Council for Culture, Hesburgh urges Catholic college educators to continue efforts to influence U.S. culture.

814.   Hinchion, Gail. "Chances for Peace Rising: Hesburgh." *South Bend Tribune*, 7 December 1988, p. A1, A17.

Hesburgh indicates that the prognosis for peace with the Soviets is rising. Hesburgh and Andrei D. Sakharov, Soviet physicist and human rights campaigner, have begun to investigate prison conditions around the world under the auspices of the Foundation for the Survival and Development of Humanity.

815.   _____. "May 5 Set for N.D. Center's Ceremonies." *South Bend Tribune*, 25 April 1988, p. B3.

Ground breaking ceremonies for the Theodore M.
Hesburgh Center for International Studies are set for
5 May 1988.

816. _____. "Cruise Leads to Plans for Notre Dame
Australia." *South Bend Tribune*, 27 November 1988.

Hesburgh guides Western Australian businessman Denis
Horgan and Peter Tannock in making plans for a
Catholic university in Australia which will be
modelled after Notre Dame, but not an affiliate.

817. Tuthill, Kelley. "Hesburgh Talks on Nuclear Arms
Race." *Observer*, 9 November 1988, p. 4.

In his lecture entitled "Prognosis for Peace,"
Hesburgh discussed the nuclear arms race, past and
present. "Our goal should be the widest conditioning
of an anti-nuclear instinct as potent as hunger."

818. Ward, Alex. "Monk Malloy's Notre Dame." *New York
Times Magazine*, 12 June 1988.

Provides a comprehensive history of Hesburgh's
accomplishments over thirty-five years at Notre Dame.
Explores Malloy's style as president in the year of
transition.

Appendix I: Special Awards and Honors Won by Theodore M. Hesburgh

Grand Cross in the Equestrian Order of the Holy Sepulchre of Jerusalem

Fellow, American Academy of Arts and Sciences

United States Navy's Distinguished Public Service Award, 1959

Medal of Freedom, 1964

Grand Gold Badge of Honor for Merits to the Republic of Austria, 1965

Antarctic Service Medal, 1968

Gold Medal, National Institute of Social Sciences, 1969

Cardinal Gibbons Medal, Catholic University of America, 1969

Bellarmine Medal, Bellarmine-Ursuline College, Louisville, 1970

Meiklejohn Award, American Association of University Professors, 1970

Charles Evans Hughes Award, National Conference of
Christians and Jews, 1970

National Catholic Educational Association Merit Award,
1971

President's Cabinet Award, University of Detroit, 1971

American Liberties Medallion, American Jewish Committee,
1971

Liberty Bell Award, Indiana State Bar Association, 1971

Clergyman of the Year Award, Religious Heritage of
America, Inc., 1972

National Law and Social Justice Leadership Award, Afro-
American Patrolmen's League of Chicago, 1972

Reinhold Niebuhr Award, 1972

Executive-of-the-Year Award, American College of
Hospital Administrators, 1973

Aquinas Award, Aquinas College, Grand Rapids, Michigan,
1973

Clark Kerr Award, Academic Senate, University of California,
Berkeley, 1973

Lyndon Baines Johnson Award, National Urban Coalition,
1973

St. Vincent de Paul Medal, DePaul University, Chicago,
1973

Profiles in Courage Award, John F. Kennedy Lodge of
B'nai B'rith, 1973

The Peter Canisius Medal, Canisius College, Buffalo,
New York, 1974

Quest Medal, St. Edward's University, Austin, Texas,
1975

National Football Foundation and Hall of Fame's
Distinguished American Award, 1975

American Institute for Public Service Award for
Greatest Public Service Benefiting the Disadvantaged,
1976

Council for Advancement and Support of Education Award
for Distinguished Service to Higher Education, 1976

Justice Award for the American Judicature Society, 1976

Herbert H. Lehman Ethics Medal, Jewish Theological
Seminary, 1976

B'nai B'rith Youth Services Gold Medallion Award for
Humanitarian Service, 1976

C. Albert Koob Merit Award, The National Catholic
Educational Association, 1977

Clergyman of the Year, The Society for the Family of
Man, 1977

First Freedom Award, Hoosier State Press Association,
1978

Hugo Black Award, University of Alabama, University,
Alabama, 1978

Grenville Clark Award, 1978

The Mary McLeod Bethune Award, U.S. Commissioner of
Education, 1979

Distinguished Service to Education Medal, The College
Board, 1980

Alexis de Tocqueville Award, United Way of America,
1980

Sylvanus Thayer Award, U.S. Military Academy, West
Point, New York, 1980

National Association of Secondary Schools Principals
Distinguished Service Award, 1981

New York University 150th Anniversary Commemorative
Award, 1981

Medal of Freedom, Fund for Higher Education, 1981

American Council on Education Annual Academic
Leadership Award, 1981

Covenant of Peace Award, Synagogue Council of America,
1981

Distinguished Service Award, Carnegie Foundation for
the Advancement of Teaching, 1981

Golden Distinguished Service Medal, Salzburg County
Government, Salzburg, Austria, 1982

Distinguished Service Award, Association of Catholic
Colleges and Universities, 1982

Jefferson Award, Council for Advancement and Support of
Education, 1982

Distinguished Service Award, American Association for
Higher Education, 1982

Liberty Award, Hebrew Immigrant Aid Society, 1983

Common Cause Public Service Achievement Award, 1984

West Georgia College Delbert Clark Award for
  Contributions to Adult and Continuing Education, 1984

Public Welfare Medal, National Academy of Sciences,
  1984

Commandeur de l'ordre des Arts et des Lettres, 1985

John De la Mennais Medal, 1985

St. Francis Xavier Medal, 1985

Sword of Loyola, Loyola University of Chicago, 1986

Department of Defense Medal for Distinguished Public
  Service, 1987

Laetare Medal, University of Notre Dame, 1987

José Matias Delgado Medal, El Salvador, 1987

Fellows of the Illinois Bar Foundation, Distinguished
  Service Award, 1988

Murray-Green-Meany Award, AFL-CIO, 1988

Charles A. Dana Award for Pioneering Achievements in
  Health and Higher Education, 1988

Compostela Award, Cathedral of St. James, Brooklyn, New
  York, 1989

Appendix II: Honorary Degrees Bestowed Upon Theodore M. Hesburgh

Le Moyne College, Syracuse, New York, 1954

Bradley University, Peoria, Illinois, 1955

Catholic University of Santiago, Chile, 1956

St. Benedict's College, Atchison, Kansas, 1958

Villanova University, Villanova, Pennsylvania, 1958

Dartmouth College, Hanover, New Hampshire, 1958

University of Rhode Island, Kingston, Rhode Island, 1960

Columbia University, New York, New York, 1961

Princeton University, Princeton, New Jersey, 1961

Brandeis University, Waltham, Massachusetts, 1962

Indiana University, Bloomington, Indiana, 1962

Northwestern University, Evanston, Illinois, 1963

Lafayette College, Easton, Pennsylvania, 1963

Honorary Citizen, University of Vienna, Austria, 1965

University of California, Los Angeles, California, 1965

St. Louis University, Baguio City, Philippines, 1965

Gonzaga University, Spokane, Washington, 1965

Temple University, Philadelphia, Pennsylvania, 1965

University of Montreal, Montreal, Canada, 1965

University of Illinois, Urbana, Illinois, 1966

Atlanta University, Atlanta, Georgia, 1966

Wabash College, Crawfordsville, Indiana, 1966

Fordham University, Bronx, New York, 1967

Manchester College, North Manchester, Indiana, 1967

Valparaiso University, Valparaiso, Indiana, 1967

Providence College, Providence, Rhode Island, 1968

University of Southern California, Los Angeles, 1968

Michigan State University, East Lansing, Michigan, 1968

Saint Mary's College, Notre Dame, Indiana, 1969

Saint Louis University, Saint Louis, Missouri, 1969

Catholic University of America, Washington, D.C., 1969

Loyola University, Chicago, Illinois, 1970

Anderson College, Anderson, Indiana, 1970

State University of New York, Albany, New York, 1970

Utah State University, Logan, Utah, 1971

Lehigh University, Bethlehem, Pennsylvania, 1971

Yale University, New Haven, Connecticut, 1971

King's College, Wilkes-Barre, Pennsylvania, 1972

Stonehill College, North Easton, Massachusetts, 1972

Alma College, Alma, Michigan, 1972

Syracuse University, Syracuse, New York, 1973

Marymount College, Tarrytown, New York, 1973

Hobart and William Smith Colleges, Geneva, New York, 1973

Hebrew Union College, Cincinnati, Ohio, 1973

Harvard University, Cambridge, Massachusetts, 1973

Regis College, Denver, Colorado, 1974

Lincoln University, Lincoln University, Pennsylvania, 1974

Tufts University, Medford, Massachusetts, 1974

The University of the South, Sewanee, Tennessee, 1974

University of Portland, Portland, Oregon, 1975

Fairfield University, Fairfield, Connecticut, 1975

Davidson College, Davidson, North Carolina, 1976

College of New Rochelle, New Rochelle, New York, 1976

University of Denver, Denver, Colorado, 1976

Beloit College, Beloit, Wisconsin, 1976

Dickinson College, Carlisle, Pennsylvania, 1977

Georgetown University, Washington, D.C., 1977

Queens College, Flushing, New York, 1977

Laval University, Quebec, Canada, 1977

Catholic University of Leuven, Leuven, Belgium,
    February 1978

Université Catholique de Louvain, Louvain-la-Neuve,
    Belgium, September 1978

University of South Carolina, Columbia, South Carolina,
    1978

University of Pennsylvania, Philadelphia, Pennsylvania,
    1978

Duquesne University, Pittsburgh, Pennsylvania, 1978

St. Francis Xavier University, Antigonish, Nova Scotia,
    1978

University of Evansville, Evansville, Indiana, 1979

Albion College, Albion, Michigan, 1979

University of Utah, Salt Lake City, Utah, 1979

Assumption College, Worcester, Massachusetts, 1979

College of William and Mary, Williamsburg, Virginia, 1980

The Johns Hopkins University, Baltimore, Maryland, 1980

Seton Hall University, South Orange, New Jersey, 1980

Tuskegee Institute, Tuskegee, Alabama, 1980

Rensselaer Polytechnic Institute, Troy, New York, 1980

University of San Diego, San Diego, California, 1980

Incarnate Word College, San Antonio, Texas, 1980

St. John Fisher College, Rochester, New York, 1981

Seattle University, Seattle, Washington, 1981

University of Toledo, Toledo, Ohio, 1981

Saint Ambrose College, Davenport, Iowa, 1981

University of Scranton, Scranton, Pennsylvania, 1981

University of Cincinnati, Cincinnati, Ohio, 1981

University of Michigan, Ann Arbor, Michigan, 1981

Hope College, Holland, Michigan, 1981

Universidade de Brasília, Brasília, Brazil, 1981

New York University, New York, New York, 1982

Indiana State University, Terre Haute, Indiana, 1982

Madonna College, Livonia, Michigan, 1982

Loyola Marymount University, Los Angeles, California, 1982

Hahnemann Medical College and Hospital, Philadelphia, Pennsylvania, 1982

Kalamazoo College, Kalamazoo, Michigan, 1982

Loretto Heights College, Denver, Colorado, 1982

Universidad Católica Madre y Maestra, Santo Domingo, Dominican Republic, 1982

Ramkhamhaeng University, Bangkok, Thailand, 1983 (in absentia)

Saint Joseph's College, Rensselaer, Indiana, 1983

Rider College, Trenton, New Jersey, 1983

Colgate University, Hamilton, New York, 1983

Immaculate Conception Seminary, Darlington, New Jersey, 1983

St. Leo's College, St. Leo, Florida, 1984

West Virginia Wesleyan College, Buckhannon, West Virginia, 1984

University of Notre Dame, Notre Dame, Indiana, 1984

Carroll College, Helena, Montana, 1985

College of Mount St. Joseph, Mount St. Joseph, Ohio,
  1985

Holy Family College, Philadelphia, Pennsylvania, 1985

Duke University, Durham, North Carolina, 1985

Christian Brothers College, Memphis, Tennessee, 1985

St. Thomas University, Fredericton, New Brunswick, 1985

Walsh College, Canton, Ohio, 1985

Briar Cliff College, Sioux City, Iowa, 1986

Aquinas College, Grand Rapids, Michigan, 1986

University of Nebraska-Lincoln, Lincoln, Nebraska, 1986

University of Pittsburgh, Pittsburgh, Pennsylvania,
  1987

University of Malta, Valletta, Malta, 1988

Rockhurst College, Kansas City, Missouri, 1988

Wheeling Jesuit College, Wheeling, West Virginia, 1989

Loyola University, New Orleans, Louisiana, 1989

Mount Saint Mary's College, Emmitsburg, Maryland, 1989

Appendix III: Current and Past Memberships on Boards and Committees Held by Theodore M. Hesburgh

Current Memberships: 1989

Mount Holyoke College, Board of Trustees

International Space University, Board of Advisors

Institute for International Peace Studies, Chairman

Kellogg Institute for International Studies, Chairman

Ecumenical Institute, Jerusalem, Chairman, Advisory Board

Institute for International Human Rights, Chairman

Institute for Ecological Research and Education, Chairman

American Committee on the French Revolution, Board of Directors

Committee on U.S.-Soviet Relations, Board

International Foundation for the Survival and Development of Humanity, Moscow, Board

Youth Service America, Board

Friends of the Institute for Democratic Alternatives
for South Africa, Board

World Harvest Council (Technoserve), Board

Center for Dialogue and Development, Advisory Council

Peace Corps Preparatory Program, Norwich College,
Northfield, Vermont, Advisory Council

Carnegie Committee on Science, Technology, and
Government, Advisory Council

World Policy Institute, Board

Great Books of the Western World, Editorial Advisor

PBS Programs--Art of Leadership, Advisory Council

National Commission on Public Service, Board

Overseas Development Council, Board

Council of Trickle-Up Programs, Member

Youth and America's Future (W. T. Grant Foundation),
Member

U.S.-China Foundation for International Exchange,
Honorary Chairman

Bretton Woods Committee, Member

American Forum, Board (Education in a Global Age)

Ploughshares, Advisory Council

National Peace Institute Foundation, Advisory Council

Jerusalem Committee, Member

Ploughshares Fund, Council

National Institute Against Prejudice and Violence,
  Advisory Board

President's Circle, National Academy of Sciences,
  Advisory Committee

U.S. Committee to Support Free Elections in Chile,
  Member

National Council of Returned Peace Corps Volunteers,
  Advisory Board

U.S.-Zululand Educational Foundation, Honorary Chairman

Lussica Video Productions, Advisory Board

U.S. Interreligious Committee for Peace in the Middle
  East, Board Member

Teachers Insurance and Annuity Association, Board of
  Trustees

Council on Foreign Relations

Institute for World Order, Honorary Chairman

Chief Executives Organization, Member

American Philosophical Society, Member

National Academy of Education, Member-at-Large

American Academy of Arts and Sciences, Member

National Committee on U.S.-China Relations, Board of
  Directors

National Advisory Board, American University,
  Washington, D.C.

Trilateral Commission, Member

National Academy of Sciences, Honorary Member

Campaign for Child Survival, Cochairman

Youth and America's Future, Commission, Member

Youth Service America, Cochairman, Development
  Committee

Inter-American Dialogue, Woodrow Wilson International
  Center for Scholars, 1982-present, Member

              Past Memberships on Boards and Committees
                 (* indicates presidential appointment)

Overseas Development Council (Chairman, 1971-1982)
  Board of Trustees

University of Jordan, Board of Trustees

National Academy of Sciences Panel on Advanced
  Technology Competition and Industrialized Allies,
  Member

*Commission on United States-Latin American Relations,
  Member

American Committee on East-West Accord, Member

National Council on Foreign Languages and International
Studies, Member

U.S. Holocaust Memorial Council, Member

Pontifical Council for Culture, Member

The Conference Board, Member

National Advisory Board, The Century Generation, Member

Fulbright Association Alumni Association Advisory
Council, Member

Committee for the Single Six-Year Presidential Term,
Member

Advisory Council on Religious Rights in Eastern Europe
and the Soviet Union, Founding Member

Sigma Xi, the Scientific Research Society, Honorary
Member

Roy Wilkins Memorial Foundation, Cochairman

Planetary Society, Advisory Board

AIDS Medical Foundation, National Council, Member

Mothers Embracing Nuclear Disarmament, National
Advisory Board, Member

National Leadership Commission on Health Care, Advisory
Group, Member

U.S.-Zululand Educational Foundation, Cochairman,
International Campaign

Rockefeller Foundation, Board of Trustees, 1961-1982
  Chairman, 1977-1982

Carnegie Fund for the Advancement of Teaching, Board of
  Trustees (later, Carnegie Commission on the Future of
  Higher Education), 1970-1976

*National Science Board, 1954-1966, Member Chairman,
  Committee on International Science

*United States Advisory Commission on International
  Educational and Cultural Affairs, 1962-1965, Member

*President's General Advisory Committee on Foreign
  Assistance Programs, Member

*President's Commission on All-Volunteer Armed Forces,
  Member

*United States Commission on Civil Rights, 1957-1972,
  Member Chairman, 1969-1972

*Presidential Clemency Board, 1974-1975, Member

Jordan Society, Member

Freedoms Foundation at Valley Forge, Board of Directors

United Negro College Fund, Inc., Board of Trustees

Council on Foreign Relations, Board of Directors and
  Chairman, Membership Committee

Harvard University Graduate School of Business
  Administration, Visiting Committee, Member

Citizen's Committee for Immigration Reform, Cochair-
  person

Business-Higher Education Forum, American Council on
  Education, Chairman

Indiana Corporation for Science and Technology, Member

Rickover Foundation, Member

International Federation of Catholic Universities,
  1963-1970, President. On Council, 1972-1975

International Atomic Energy Agency, Vatican City
  Permanent Representative, 1957-1970

International Association of Universities, Deputy
  Member, Administrative Board, 1970-1975

American Bar Association Commission on Campus
  Government and Student Dissent

Rockefeller Brothers Fund, Special Studies Group

*State Department's Policy Planning Council, Member

Select Committee on the Future of Private and
  Independent Higher Education in New York State, Member

*National War College, Board of Consultants

*United States Naval Academy, Board of Visitors, Member
  and Chairman

Association of American Colleges, Past President

American Council on Education, Board of Directors

Woodrow Wilson National Fellowship Foundation, Board of
  Trustees

Institute of International Education, Board of
  Trustees; Member, Council on Higher Education in the

American Republics and Executive Board of CHEAR, 1963-1970

Universities Research Association, Council of Presidents

Argonne National Laboratory, Policy Advisory Board

Ford Motor Company Fund, Scholarship Board, Member

General Motors Corporation, Scholarship Board, Member

Young Presidents Organization

Tulane University, Board of Visitors

Ecumenical Institute for Advanced Theological Studies
in Jerusalem, Chairman, Academic Council

Nutrition Foundation, Board of Trustees

*United Nations Conference on Science and Technology
for Development, 1979, United States Ambassador

Cambodian Crisis Committee, Cochairman, 1979-1980

*President's Commission on the Holocaust, until 1980

Chase Manhattan Bank, Board of Directors, until 1981

*Select Commission on Immigration and Refugee Policy,
Chairman, 1979-1981

*U.S. Official Observer Team for El Salvador Elections,
March 1982, Member

Index

Works are indexed by author, title, and subject. References preceded by p. or pp. refer to page numbers. All other references are to item numbers in the bibliography.

ABOUT THE COMPILER AND BIOGRAPHER

CHARLOTTE AMES is Bibliographer of Catholic Americana at the Theodore M. Hesburgh Library, University of Notre Dame. In 1989, with Thomas J. Mueller, she compiled *Commitment, Compassion, Consecration: Inspirational Quotes of Theodore M. Hesburgh, C.S.C.* She has also compiled other works relevant to the study of American Catholic History.

THOMAS STRITCH is Professor Emeritus of American Studies at the University of Notre Dame. He is former editor and currently associate editor of *The Review of Politics,* was coeditor of *The New Corporatism* (1974) and author of *The Catholic Church in Tennessee: The Sesquicentennial Story* (1987).